Crucial Mentoring Conversations

Endorsements

If you think you understand how to be an effective mentor, read again. *Crucial Mentoring Conversations* is the most comprehensive and engaging book on mentoring I've ever experienced. Niël Steinmann's circle of eight essential questions—from Purpose to Performance—comes with a template that works for all of them, plus thought-provoking examples that work for each of them. I've been mentoring for years. I'll be mentoring differently because of Steinmann's actionable insights.

Tom Pierce, President Pierce Management Development, Washington, D.C.

I have had the privilege of seeing Niël in action over the years. As the CEO of Deloitte Consulting in Southern Africa, I asked Niël to assist with an intervention to ensure there was synergy in the leadership team. Little did I realise that the success we achieved as a team was as a result of the conversations and questions we started asking ourselves with Niël's gentle prompting. In this book on mentorship, in his own style Niël expands on the life and business altering questions that have to be asked. Only after reading his insightful book did I realise that Niël was using mentoring conversations to drive personal leadership development, which directly contributed to the achievement of our collective BHAG (Big Hairy Audacious Goals) as a team and individually.

I see enormous value in using this practical guide – for leaders to shape conversations with those they want to inspire and develop, and for those who are looking for ways to formalise discussions with people they want to learn from. By reading this book, I was reminded of the importance to put back as a means to say thank you for all those who invested in me over the years. After all, that is the only thing one will be remembered for. As Disraeli said, "the greatest good you can do for another is not just share your riches, but to reveal to him his own."

Louis Geeringh, Group Chief Executive Officer
Capitalworks Investment Partners (Pty) Limited

This book provides great insights shared by Niël who has been instrumental in spearheading the start of many successful mentoring relationships amongst senior and executive leaders. The book is also structured in a way that allows the reader to easily follow what he is sharing.

For those who may still be skeptical or hesitant about stepping into a mentoring relationship, possibly due to uncertainty about how to take the relationship forward or hold a meaningful and constructive conversation with a mentee, this step-by-step crucial conversation process serves as a useful guide for navigating the mentoring relationship.

Crucial Mentoring Conversations is a book that will set a compass for the mentoring relationship for mentor and mentee alike.

> *Robert Goff, Chief Executive: Human Resources Sanlam Personal Finance*

As my Dad used to say, "Always listen to a voice with experience". I can truly state that in my 27 years as a Human Resources professional, I've never come across a book with so much insight into what it really means to be a mentor who can influence or play a significant role in someone's life, be it on a personal or business level. The way in which Niël writes about this sometimes complex topic has to be commended, as it is presented in a user-friendly/logical manner that makes it easy to grasp and apply, even to the lay man out there; it is practical with so much insight and truth.

This is a remarkable and must read for all managers/leaders out there who want to make this world a better place for all, especially in the workplace. It is a brilliant piece of work in that it is close to what is needed in the South African working environment, especially with the future in mind and the challenges we are facing. I sincerely believe that the author has made it clear that it's time for business to start facing the music and start doing what matters the most; that it is about the mentees and investing in their future, adding value to time. Niël, thanks for sharing your own personal experiences, it makes it so much more significant and relevant. You've highlighted that sometimes we shouldn't just take things for granted, and in your own words, "For me, mentoring is a way of life, a passion and a profession". Wow!

> *Stephen de Beer, Human Resources Executive Forever Resorts SA*

I have had the pleasure of working with Niël since 2004 and have yet to find someone as passionate and intentional about mentorship. His use of the analogy of a lioness raising her cubs best illustrates the magic that is mentoring, and I see this book as a natural extension of his work. This is a handy go-to guide for mentors, which provides tools, crucial conversation guides and talent perspectives that are appropriate and practical.

In this VUCA world we find ourselves in, relationships are the key to success in life. The return on relationships is the new currency and what better way to invest than through mentorship, with a clearly defined end in mind that provides reciprocal outcomes. I recommend it for all corporate leaders who want to bring meaning to their individual and corporate purpose.

> *Celeste Bennett, Talent and Development Manager Engen*

Being a pracademic, I opt to invest in resources which enable practitioners to apply solid practice underpinned by sound and relevant theory. What I found in this powerful resource is a practical structure for crucial and often uncomfortable conversations, which leaves room for choice with regard to approach and interpretation, whilst it is clear about intentionality and accountability. Its core value lies in the wisdom that Niël has co-created with individuals and teams over many years of intense and successful work as a mentor, facilitator and enabler of transformation. The focus on narrative spans not just cultures but also borders, and reinforces the value of investing in partnerships that are underpinned by mutual respect and focused on lifelong learning.

Dr. Salome van Coller-Peter, Team Coach and Learning Facilitator

Niël's first book, *Raising Giant Killers*, changed the way I viewed mentoring and ignited a passion in me to mentor young engineers. *Crucial Mentoring Conversations* is an excellent addition to Niël's work in this area. It focuses on the most challenging component of mentoring, i.e. creating an authentic relationship built on a foundation of trust. The most challenging aspect of mentoring millennials is the ability to build and maintain an authentic relationship. Niël's book presents an excellent tool set to enable real conversations between mentor and mentee. The approach is focused on real, authentic relationship building. This work unpacks effective methods to tackle very difficult but crucial conversations with the aim of building a foundation of trust. I truly believe that the tools presented will strengthen existing mentor/mentee relationships and will create levels of mutual trust and respect that could exist for a lifetime.

Keith Johnston, Engineering Systems Manager Chevron, Houston, TX

Niël has been closely involved with our organisation for a number of years, implementing mentoring solutions across different organisational levels of work.

We have successfully implemented Niël's framework of crucial conversations with mentors, mentees and leadership teams in various contexts of talent development. The framework of conversations has proven to be a powerful tool in facilitating learning, insight and institutional alignment. It has allowed mentors to better structure their mentoring conversations and to facilitate meaningful discussion by asking the right questions.

Crucial Mentoring Conversations is an easy read and a practical handbook filled with helpful tools and ample reference notes. Each of the eight conversation topics are structured to provide the reader with the necessary context to the topic; sample questions; mentoring metaphors relevant to the topic; as well as the envisaged outcome.

This book will most definitely enable honest and courageous conversations in both personal and professional relationships!

Colette Wessels, HR Director Imperial Health Sciences

Excellent! A wealth of knowledge, insights and practical tips. This book is a must read for all leaders and managers who are dedicated to building a high performance culture. Anyone with a passion to help colleagues reach their potential will benefit from this book. A broad spectrum of topics, content and references, including valuable "need to knows". Thank you Niël for sharing your expertise and experience with us.

Anja van Beek, VP People Africa Middle East, Asia & Australia, People Function Sage

Many mentors have a spirit of generosity, wanting to impart their knowledge and make a difference in the life of another, yet the practicality of conducting mentoring discussions is often experienced as quite daunting. Niël's book is an invaluable tool, providing helpful guidelines to generate the in-depth and meaningful conversations that are most likely to result in rich learning experiences for both mentors and mentees.

Estelle Coetzer, Industrial & Organisational Psychologist GreyQ Consulting

Niël Steinman is notorious for using the depictions in wild life to visualize powerful business lessons. Here he has once again distinguished himself as an author, successfully encapsulating a comprehensive approach towards mentoring. His approach is practical, different, powerful and unique.

Crucial conversations, the central theme of the book reflects the strategic role of mentoring in business. Business is all about winning, return on investment and maximizing equity. The future of business lies in the hands of the Millennials; however, they grew up in a society focused on instant gratification while settling for mediocrity resulting in "unconscious incompetence". Therefor the challenge for any business is to convert this unintentional cognitive disposition into "unconscious competence". To capitalize on the wealth of energy and human capital provided by the entrance of the millennium population will distinguish business success in the future. It starts with facilitating crucial conversations through structured mentoring programs today.

Peter van der Linde, Vice President, Retail Operations Mark's, Calgary, Canada

Copyright © KR Publishing and Niël Steinmann

All reasonable steps have been taken to ensure that the contents of this book do not, directly or indirectly, infringe any existing copyright of any third person and, further, that all quotations or extracts taken from any other publication or work have been appropriately acknowledged and referenced. The publisher, editors and printers take no responsibility for any copyright infringement committed by an author of this work.

Copyright subsists in this work. No part of this work may be reproduced in any form or by any means without the written consent of the publisher or the author.

While the publisher, editors and printers have taken all reasonable steps to ensure the accuracy of the contents of this work, they take no responsibility for any loss or damage suffered by any person as a result of that person relying on the information contained in this work.

First published in 2017

ISBN: 978-1-86922-670-1
eISBN: 978-1-86922-671-8 (ePDF)

Published by KR Publishing
P O Box 3954
Randburg
2125
Republic of South Africa

Tel: (011) 706-6009
Fax: (011) 706-1127
E-mail: orders@knowres.co.za
Website: www.kr.co.za

Printed and bound: HartWood Digital Printing, 243 Alexandra Avenue, Halfway House, Midrand
Typesetting, layout and design: Cia Joubert, cia@knowres.co.za
Cover design: Louise van der Westhuizen, LoveLab, louise@lovelab.co.za
Editing & proofreading: Jennifer Renton, jenniferrenton@live.co.za
Project management: Cia Joubert, cia@knowres.co.za
Index created with TExtract / www.Texyz.com

Crucial Mentoring Conversations

by

Niël Steinmann

2017

Dedication

For Daneel and Stephan. My own giant killers!

Table of Contents

Acknowledgements v
Foreword by Ruby Motloheloa vi
About the Author ix
Preface x
Introduction and thoughts on how to use this book xii

Part 1 The world of mentoring 1

Mentoring and coaching 2
Mentoring today 4
Peer mentoring 5
A generational view on mentoring 6
The value of reverse mentoring 8
Formal vs informal mentoring 10
The value-add of mentoring in business 11
The challenges of structured or formal mentoring 12
    What is the purpose of formal mentoring in your business? 14
    Who should be mentors? 14
    How should you match mentors and mentees? 15
    Does the success of formal mentoring depend on the mentee? 16
    How do you sustain a formal mentoring relationship? 17
    How much structure is necessary? 17
The need to be more intentional as mentors 19
    Nurturing a profitable relationship 19
    The formation of the relationship 20
    Intentional mentors ensure that their mentees become
    "definitively competent" 21
    Mentors could contribute to both the technical and professional
    competence of the mentee 21
    Mentors should inspire and influence the appropriate
    "mindset" 22

Mentors must reveal the need for institutional alignment............. 23
Mentors should convey the 'territorial wisdom' 23
Mentors should help encourage their mentees to focus 24
Being intentional about the 70-20-10 25
Provide blended learning to increase the impact of formal learning.................. 26
Create collaborative learning environments 26
Leveraging intentional mentoring.................. 27

Part 2 An introduction to crucial mentoring conversations............ 29

A personal experience.................. 30
Demystifying crucial mentoring conversations 31
The purpose of a crucial mentoring conversation 32
Ingredients of successful crucial mentoring conversations 34
    Turn down the noise.................. 34
    Reciprocal contributions from both parties.................. 36
    Authentic trust in each other and in the purpose of the relationship 37
    Resulting actions/assignments that come to light through these conversations 42
The topics that crucial mentoring conversations can/should cover 42
Who should own or drive these conversations?.................. 43
When should you have a crucial conversation? 44
Creating success at having crucial mentoring conversations 47
    The power of storytelling… "A long time ago in a galaxy far, far away".................. 48
    When is storytelling powerful?.................. 49
    When you have a story to tell about yourself.................. 49
    When you want to share a particular lesson 49
    When you need to illustrate a moral or ethical issue.................. 49
    When you want to communicate across boundaries (culture, gender, religion, generation).................. 50
    When you want to share a truth 50
    Three critical aspects of stories to remember.................. 50

Ensure honesty and safety in your conversations 51
    The sweet aroma of authenticity 52
    How can mentors ensure greater authenticity? 52
At what stage should confrontation be part of a crucial mentoring
    conversation? 56
    Observe 57
    Articulate 57
    Validate 57
    The power of questioning 58
How to end a crucial mentoring conversation 58
    The importance of action and execution 59

Part 3 Guiding and leading crucial mentoring conversations 62

Conversation on purpose and vision 65
    Uncovering purpose and values 67
    Linking individual and corporate purpose 67
    Creating a personal life timeline 70
    Reflecting on values 72

Conversation on career momentum/mobility 74
    Understanding the challenge of employability 74
    Why do people get promoted? 76
    Discovering career anchors 80

Conversation on performance 83
    Work performance 84
    Rethinking performance – challenging the performance
        management paradigm 86
    Useful pointers on feedback 87

Conversation on fitness 89
    Prerequisites for fitness conversations 92
    Does your organisation calibrate talent/fitness? 92

Conversation on strengths 96
    So what about your mentee's weaknesses? 99

Conversation on relationships 101
    The Johari window 103
    Taking the sting out of conflict 105

Conversation on networks 110
    Embrace the 'meeting before the meeting' principle 113
    Create a network mapping chart 113
    The dangers of social networking 115

Conversation on classified issues 117

Part 4 Pouring yourself into someone 121

Mentoring high performers 122
Challenging comfort zones with the best intentions 126
Recognise when to "go off-line" 128
The most common mistakes that mentors make 129
    Low expectations for the mentee? 129
    Mentors acting as guides 129
    Underestimating the effort 130
    Hiding your mistakes 130
    Not managing expectations 130
Evaluating the impact of your crucial mentoring conversations 131
In conclusion 132
References 137
Index 138

Acknowledgements

This book is the product of the combined wisdom of mentors who I have met and worked with for over 25 years. My thanks to all of you for enriching my understanding of, and passion for, mentoring.

I would particularly like to thank:

all the parents, schools, non-profit organisations and corporate institutions that have trusted me to share, to learn, and to explore the wonder of mentoring;

my colleagues at PDD, who have been instrumental in providing valuable collaboration and feedback;

my Mom, who laid the foundation and invested so much in me as a person;

my lovely wife, who has always prayed with, encouraged and supported me;

all those who gave their valuable time to endorse this book;

thank you to Louise from LoveLab for the design of the cover and conversation icons;

the Knowledge Resources staff for the editing, layout and marketing of the book; and

Cia Joubert for the publication.

Foreword by Ruby Motloheloa

The concepts of mentoring and coaching are often used interchangeably, informally and casually within the workplace and academic circles. In part one of *Crucial Mentoring Conversations*, Niël provides a holistic view of mentoring, starting with a very clear distinction between mentoring and coaching. This includes the professional, academic and practical definitions and applications of coaching and mentoring. The outline and emphasis of the "DNA of a mentor" challenges the traditional view of the mentor as the expert whose role is primarily to guide, advise and develop the mentee. Niël highlights specific attributes that challenge us in the field of people development to critically re-examine the criteria of selecting mentors. Fundamentally, this also challenges mentors to evaluate how they measure up. It is also clear that the process of mentoring has evolved to highlight the significance of the various, interchangeable roles of line managers, peers, formal mentors, mentors and subordinates. This brings a significant dynamism to the mentoring process and calls for a critical re-evaluation of mentorship programmes as well as the critical success factors attached to them. Niël's generational view on mentoring, as well as his emphasis on reverse mentoring, offers an empowering perspective to anyone seeking to optimise the impact and value of the mentoring process for those involved in mentoring relationships and their sponsors, as well as for the organisations within which these mentoring relationships are implemented.

Niël emphasises and very clearly outlines that the success and effectiveness of any mentoring relationship and process is not inherent in the role of the line manager, but rather requires a different breed of mentors who are in the business of multiplying others and facilitating a process of making others stand out and shine even brighter than themselves. This necessitates unique qualities in those selected to fulfil the role of mentor, with authenticity and humility being two of these attributes. However success not only relies on the attributes of the mentor but the mentee as well. Niël positions mentoring as being fundamentally relational in nature, and thus the role and qualities of the mentee are equally critical to the success of the relationship. Furthermore, those of us responsible for establishing and implementing mentoring programmes in our organisations are a critical stakeholder in the mentoring relationship. Niël challenges how mentoring is positioned and describes the need to create an environment that is conducive for crucial conversations within the mentoring relationship as being the core driver of the mentoring process. These conversations cannot be superficial; they require commitment, intent and continuous reflections by mentors, mentees and custodians of people development as part of a continuous journey of learning, growth and development for all parties.

Niël kick-starts part two of the book by sharing reflections of his personal journey, highlighting a profound conversation with one of his informal mentors that shaped his career. He goes on to demystify crucial mentoring conversations by highlighting the nature of these conversations and outlining how these conversations positively and effectively impact the mentee's personal and professional life.

According to Niël, there are specific ingredients which serve as prerequisites for an effective crucial mentoring conversations, and he elaborates on these. Furthermore, it outlines factors and techniques for successful mentoring.

Part three of the book explores the nature and value of purposeful, focused, principle-centred conversations that begin with an end in mind and are driven by values. Niël offers practical guides and techniques for effective crucial mentoring conversations. He also shares some real questions for mentors to explore about the conversations with their mentees, as well as areas to focus on that will make these conversations meaningful.

Part four of the book focuses on the aspects of mentoring that are of crucial importance in relation to the overall effectiveness of mentoring. These include issues such as mentoring high achievers who are ambitious, competitive and self-assured. This part of the book re-emphasises which skills and techniques are needed to support and guide mentors to make and facilitate an effective and impactful learning process for their mentees.

I was affectionately drawn to various concepts discussed in the book, as I reflected on my experience in a formal mentoring process back in 1997 when I was selected to participate in an accelerated leadership development programme as a young, emerging, African female facing challenges within the corporate world, and deeply questioning whether the white male recommended as my mentor was the right person for the role. Needless to say, this very relationship gave a significant boost to my professional and personal journey. This was purely because the relationship with my mentor was marked by mutual authentic trust, self-exploration and awareness, as well as an openness from my mentor to receive constructive feedback and learn from me. My mentor took a genuine interest in my character and professional development and he truly cared and demonstrated genuine interest in me. I can still recall some of the endless conversations we had, which moved me to think deeper about my purpose, relationships, the challenges I was facing at the time and my overall personal brand and effectiveness. I remember approaching my mentor seeking a solution after being unfairly treated within the organisation and I vividly recall walking away from him with no immediate solution but challenging questions that I had to reflect on about me, what I truly wanted, and how to best respond to my current circumstances in a way that would serve my purpose. This man was Niël Steinmann. That relationship achieved its purpose at the time, as it positioned me as an emerging leader and one of the first in my group to be formally appointed into a leadership role. The formal mentoring relationship ended, standing out as one of the most successful relationships in the group.

This sparked a relationship which evolved through the years into a meaningful professional partnership, with Niël implementing crucial mentoring conversations in South Africa and other businesses on the continent within a multinational business where I was head of learning and organisational development. I can thus personally attest to the meaningful, impactful and effective role of these crucial conversations in mentoring relationships.

Crucial Mentoring Conversations is a must read for anyone who seeks to make a meaningful impact on the development of others.

Ruby Motloheloa
HRD Manager, Tiger Brands

About the author

Niël Steinmann is a specialist business consultant and registered Industrial Psychologist, who has spent more than 25 years studying mentoring, coaching and leadership development. In 1999 he founded People's Dynamic Development, a management consultancy that utilises African analogies to develop people and organisations to significantly increase their performance capacity.

In addition to his consulting work, Niël has a passion for nature and is a keen conservationist, with a special interest in lions. His close interactions with lions led him to author his first book, *Fundamentals for effective mentoring: Raising giant killers*, which shares a powerful metaphor and case for sustainable mentoring relationships. The book received international recognition and endorsements from the renowned leadership consultant, Dr. Ken Blanchard.

Furthermore, Niël's contributions to notable South African and international companies has resulted in him being recognised and respected for his ground-breaking work in the social sectors, including education, healthcare, faith-based organisations, entrepreneurial ventures and non-profit organisations. He is also a regular speaker at local and international conferences.

Niël is described by friends as a struggling golfer, a passionate cyclist, a proud father and a loving husband.

Preface

Mentoring has been a personal experience that has been evident throughout my career. I can truly say that I am who I am because of others who have cared for, inspired and invested in me as a person. Some of these remarkable individuals have passed on, leaving a distinct mark on my life, while others, after many years, are still ploughing away, pouring their time and passion into my personal journey. My married life, our efforts to raise our two remarkably gifted and talented boys, my stint as a corporate citizen, and my time as entrepreneur starting a new business venture and now CEO of a management consultancy, are all testament to profitable mentoring relationships.

During the last 18 years I have had the pleasure of pursuing my passion in life, working with some of the top business firms in the world and meeting thousands of their highly talented staff on different continents. All these organisations were committed to create effective mentoring cultures and were willing to sponsor their employees to advance their careers and develop themselves both personally and professionally. During this time I experienced different approaches and changes to how mentoring is viewed and implemented, and I have witnessed some truly remarkable mentoring relationships.

I have also pursued another great passion. As an amateur conservationist, I have studied lions both in nature and captivity for nearly 20 years. This unique experience allowed me to learn from these great beasts, and in doing so I discovered a powerful metaphor for business and for mentors and mentees alike.

These fascinating animals taught me many lessons on strategy, leadership, effective communication and teamwork. I also studied how a lioness raises her cubs to maturity, which provided an opportunity to write my first book, *Fundamentals for effective mentoring: Raising giant killers*.

My personal mission and those of my colleagues is to create a world where the value of mentoring is recognised and copiously leveraged. Our world needs more leaders at all levels of society, with people being treated with respect and dignity. We need to become better human beings before we become good doctors, great teachers, gifted accountants, successful entrepreneurs or recognised sport stars.

Authentic mentoring relationships in my view contribute to our society as a whole. ***As much as mentors leave something behind, they help shape a better future for us all! Mentoring relationships, in a much broader context, create sustainability for the future of our families, communities, organisations and country.***

Introduction and thoughts on how to use this book

Throughout history mentors have been political advisors, strategic thinkers, thriving business personalities, outstanding educators, religious leaders, sporting icons and loving parents. They have all performed this multi-faceted role informally, simply because of their passion and belief in those in whom they have invested their time.

Yet informal mentoring has failed to keep up with trends in business; mentoring is now a strategic business initiative and institutions are more than ever expecting to see a "return on relationship". It is for this reason that organisations have been tempted to structure and formalise mentoring. Mentors are tasked with this "professional obligation", often without any road map to show them where the journey might go, and yet these relationships are expected to extract greater value-add for mentees' growth and development! We should, first of all, recognise that formal/structured mentoring really grew from observing the unquestionable benefits that resulted from those first authentic mentoring relationships, which were the result of a natural affinity between two people.

Over the years, I have noticed that the most successful mentoring relationships are those that grow organically, where there is a natural attraction between mentor and mentee. A mentor who has travelled this road will confirm that each and every mentoring relationship is different, with its own fresh set of challenges. Modern mentoring requires more than an ad hoc effort where mentors and mentees get together for a cup of coffee; rather, mentees benefit from a more deliberate effort by mentors who are intentional in their conversations, the opportunities they provide, and the feedback they give.

The complexity of our world and the sheer pace of change force us to position modern mentoring as a premeditated effort in families, schools, communities, churches, volunteer groups, and non-profit and profit making institutions/organisations.

The success of a more structured/formal mentoring relationship (like any other) depends on both parties' commitment to meeting the challenges of the relationship and to take full advantage of the opportunities that are presented – all of this with a clear end in mind for the relationship!

This book is written to provide a framework for all prospective mentors who would like to fulfil a more intentional mentoring role, but who are also conscious of the challenges that a formal or structured relationship bring.

How you use the book is up to you. I would encourage using it with your mentees, within your leadership team, or even with mentoring peers, talking through the conversations I have provided or making up your own. See it as a framework to be more intentional as a mentor. It is written to provide insight into various crucial conversations so that you can facilitate awareness and learning in ways that enrich, challenge, inspire and enable your mentee to learn about themselves and their world.

You might like to apply the book's content to your organisation's thinking around career and succession conversations, but you will note that the book is written independently of organisational affiliation – it has no institutional boundaries! The book is most definitely not the ultimate mentoring guide. I have not included the steps that an organisation needs to take, thoughts on how to match a mentor to a mentee, how to put a well-structured agreement in place, or the detail of the phases of a more formal mentoring relationship. Rather, it is written to facilitate intimate conversations between a mentor and mentee in a variety of settings.

I am big on questions; the right questions have had a profound impact on my life, which is why I have included questions as part of each of the crucial conversations. This book will present you with a collection of practical questions, steps and strategies for reflection and action.

You could use the questions for the various crucial conversations to prepare in advance of your mentoring sessions. These questions are meant to be helpful cues that serve as a guide. Honour your mentee's learning style and consider the agreed amount of structure that you would like to deploy in the relationship, however, as we all learn in different ways. Some conversations and supplemental questions will engage your mentee and others won't. You might like to work through the conversations yourself as well as with your mentee. I would also like you to consider your own mentoring journey. Who is on your board of trustees? Do you have "profitable" learning relationships, and more importantly, are you making an intentional effort to invest in the lives of others?

Remember mentors never stop mentoring – that is the difference between success and significance. In John Maxwell's words, "Success is when I add value to my life. Significance is when I add value to others … I think mentoring is significance…".

Part 1
The world of mentoring

Mentoring and coaching

The terms, mentoring and coaching, are often used synonymously, which has potentially contributed to the confusion around these practices. Having worked in both fields over the last 20 years, and given the fact that I have visited several countries where mentoring and coaching are practiced, I need to emphasise that a simplistic generalised classification and/or differentiation of mentoring/coaching is problematic. The biggest mistake individuals and companies make is to over-simplify the differences between the two, which invariably leads to a mentoring versus coaching approach that unfortunately negates the richness of both approaches. The reality is that there are many different types and variations of mentoring and coaching, and these different methodologies cannot be easily categorised within a specific professional bodies definition. I will, however, attempt to highlight some key elements of both practices.

In contrast to the superficial definitions provided in most literature, mentoring and coaching can be either directional or non-directional, depending on the need, context and unique circumstances of a specific relationship, the nature of the tasks to be performed, the organisation, or the industry.

The International Coach Federation describes coaching as, "an ongoing partnership that helps clients to produce fulfilling results in their personal and professional lives. Through the process of coaching, clients deepen their learning, improve their performance and enhance their quality of life".

COMENSA defines coaching as "a professional, collaborative and outcomes-driven method of learning that seeks to develop an individual and raise self-awareness so that he might achieve specific goals and perform at a more effective level". This means that coaches partner with their clients in a thought-provoking and creative process to maximise their potential both personally and professionally.

Coaches might emphasise new competencies, learning and goal attainment. Everything in coaching hinges on listening with the client's agenda in mind and then responding with appropriate questions that allow the client to explore possibilities.

Coaching has evolved professionally and could include:

- **Executive coaching** aims to inspire executive leaders to make behavioural changes that will benefit people and improve results and business performance. It also offers leaders a clearer understanding of their roles and responsibilities. When leaders are more confident about what they need to do, they are better able to motivate employees and mobilise them for action.

- **Business coaches** work with small and medium sized enterprises with the specific focus of growing the organisation and the client as an individual.

- **Workplace coaching** allows managers to equip their staff with the knowledge, tools, and skills to fulfil their jobs. They understand that confidence comes from competence. The applications of workplace coaching can vary, from support to achieve a specific project, to helping an individual improve their skill levels, to developing a necessary skill.

- **Life coaching** is a practice that aims to help clients determine and achieve their personal goals. The coach will work with the client and focus on a variety of aspects that they want to achieve. This could include work challenges, personal relationships, health and/or finances.

The term 'mentoring' has been around for centuries. It originates from Greek mythology when King Ulysses, leaving for the city of Troy, asked his friend Mentor to take care of his son and to become his teacher, advisor and guardian. From this history it confirms that mentoring could therefore be both instructional and advice-giving.

David Clutterbuck is of the opinion that, "A mentor is normally a more experienced individual willing to share knowledge and insights with someone less experienced in a relationship of mutual trust". We will later explore the notion that less experienced individuals can also mentor more experienced individuals.

The DNA of a mentor revolves around a "heart" for others, a spirit of generosity and a passion for a specific discipline or skill. Mentors savour the moments when those in whose lives they invest, achieve their dreams and taste their own success of their endeavours; they have a benevolent presence without having to act in an authoritarian way.

Steven Spielberg, the famous film director, explains that mentoring is "a delicate balance, not to create in your own image, but to give others the opportunity to create themselves".

Mentors pass on specific knowledge and life experiences. They offer insight and guidance but also have the ability to stretch and challenge those in pursuit of their dreams. They could potentially sponsor development opportunities or merely connect individuals within their network.

For some, mentors are role models who cleared the way through their actions and achievements, while for others, mentors are individuals who can be trusted, who are authentic and honest, and who will ultimately hold them accountable for their actions and decisions. The success of mentoring lies in the quality of the relationship. In the past, mentoring evolved in a spontaneous way. Informal interactions possibly contributed to a mutual attraction between mentor and mentee that allowed the relationship to organically grow. Mentees frequently testify to the impact that mentors had in their lives, often without any evidence of a formalised or structured relationship.

Mentoring today

Mentoring is more on the agenda now than ever before. According to Ellen Ensher, Associate Professor of Management at the business college at Loyola Marymount University in Los Angeles, three out of four *Fortune* 500 firms have formal mentoring programmes. Businesses see corporate mentoring programmes as being crucial to employee engagement, talent management and development, particularly in highly skilled careers. People who use mentors are more successful than those without mentors, a fact that has been substantiated by academic research. They get more promotions, make more money, and have more career and job satisfaction.

Your boss is most definitely not your only mentor. Mentors are all around us today. Your peers with whom you work and practice, and even subordinates, could play a significant role. We are constantly learning from others, as the reality is that no one person can have all the answers. Social media and virtual platforms continue to accelerate the pace of learning, while increased globalisation highlights the complexities of our world. The pace of change means that no one is qualified enough for us to entrust our career expectations and development journey to a single or lifelong mentor. Consider the uniqueness of the learner, the complexities of the brain and Emotional Intelligence – all of these should bring fundamental changes to mentoring.

The learning process has shifted from mentor directed to self-directed, while the goals of mentoring have shifted from knowledge transfer to critical reflection and application. Your mentee will no longer be a passive recipient but an active learner, and you as a mentor are no longer an authority figure but a facilitator of learning. Let us challenge the paradigm; mentoring is no longer a one-on-one, formalised, face-to-face practice where an older/wiser person grooms a younger mentee for a specific job.

Understanding the value of the different types of mentoring relationships is useful to fully explore the benefits of mentoring today.

Peer mentoring

There are several reasons why peer mentoring has grown over the years. Learners respect the views of their peers who might be just one or two steps ahead of them in terms of experience or proficiency. The opportunity to collaborate with peers in your own network allows for greater contextual understanding. Because they live the same reality and face similar challenges and demanding situations, peers understand the culture, work pressures, realties and complexities, which potentially make them the best sources for social support and encouragement. Added to this, there is probably a more established bond with those close to you, as well as the fact that these peers are more accessible and available than some senior subject matter expert or leader, which makes them the ideal 'go to' option for the young professional/manager.

Some organisations and institutions have managed to increase their employees' confidence and competencies by providing platforms for peers to connect across the business. Those who have leveraged peer mentoring confirm greater support networks, better contextual understanding and improved competencies and skills sets.

The value of peer mentoring is possibly misunderstood because of the traditional mentoring paradigm.

A generational view on mentoring

It would be appropriate to have an understanding of the various terms used in literature. The term 'Baby boomer' refers to the generation born after the Second World War, from 1946 to the early 1960s. Generation X is the next generation, who were born between 1961 and 1981, followed by the Millennials or Gen Y, between 1981 and 1995. The generation after the Millennials will be called 'Gen Z', who were born after 1995. They will be the most technologically literate generation thus far.

Most of us can recall that the initial focus of the information age was to gather information and make the content available. Google the words 'mentoring' or 'knowledge sharing' and note the millions of links and results that are immediately available. Information overload is a reality and a great concern, as the world that we are living in requires a lot more than the mere gathering of information to be successful. In today's knowledge economy, workers need a great deal more tacit information and insight into how to apply knowledge on the job.

The true value of mentoring lies in connecting with those who can provide insights and experiences that are not captured in some policy document or procedure. Mentoring as a development tool is embraced by Millennials, as they view it as the way life works. They are no longer the leaders of tomorrow but the leaders of today!

Millennials place a strong emphasis on finding work that is personally fulfilling. They want work to afford them the opportunity to establish new relationships, learn new skills, and identify with a larger purpose. Sense of purpose is a critical factor in their quest for job satisfaction, and is one of the crucial mentoring conversations that will be discussed in this book.

Millennials also view continuous learning as important to their future success. Their exposure to ever changing technology has forced them to adapt and become proficient at sourcing and using the latest innovations. They join organisations where the opportunity for personal development is a top priority.

Table 1: What millennials want

To learn	From their manager	From their company
Technical skills and expertise	Plotting a career path	Developing future skills
Leadership skills	On the job coaching and mentoring	Strong company values
Industry specific knowledge (big picture)	Honest feedback on performance	Work/life balance and a flexible environment

To learn	From their manager	From their company
Self-management and emotional intelligence	Sponsoring formal development opportunities	Support for their leadership ambitions
Business and entrepreneurial skills	Provide exposure to the managers' networks	To be fully utilised
Navigating a career	Understand big picture thinking	Connect to the organisational purpose

A recent global survey on Millennials conducted by Deloitte suggests that Millennials want mentors who are accessible and available, who show a genuine interest in their development, who can offer quality advice, and who exhibit listening skills that will build trusting relationships.

In summary, mentoring the younger generations will require more informal (yet structured) efforts, which are more relational and value-based. These prerequisites dovetail with the thinking that suggest that mentors who are intentional can facilitate/lead specific crucial mentoring conversations.

The value of reverse mentoring

Reverse mentoring was championed by Jack Welch when he was chief executive of General Electric Co. He encouraged 500 top-level executives to reach out to junior staff members below them to learn how to use the Internet. Jack himself was matched with an employee in her 20s who taught him how to surf the Web. Fast forward more than a decade and reverse mentoring (or reciprocal mentoring) gives young, entry-level, often 'tech-competent', employees the chance to 'educate' senior members of staff about business interests such as trends and utilities in social media (these skills are now becoming increasingly valuable), new technology, customer preferences and unusual methods to boost office morale.

The result? Mentoring relationships that shift into reverse before they move forward. When mentors interact with their younger team members, even those who might be younger than their own children, it is a guaranteed eye-opener.

In addition to exposure on the latest social media platforms, reverse mentoring can also give the manager/leader more candid feedback than any 360 degree programme. Sometimes a younger and more junior person hasn't learned what they can't say, they have fresh eyes and fresh ears, and they can provide honest feedback on perceptions around leadership style – even opinions and views that others might find tough to express. They will say and share things because they haven't "carried the corporate baggage yet". No doubt, younger, fresher eyes will see things differently than we will. Their insights might even be shocking, and if we can keep our egos in check, they could lead to powerful breakthroughs.

A further benefit of reverse mentoring initiatives is that they provide managers with insights into team members' expectations and aspirations, allowing the organisation to foster a culture designed to keep them motivated and engaged as they become the next generation of leaders in the workplace.

Here are some possible topics for reverse mentoring relationships:

- Operational insights, products, ideas and plans.
- Angles on diversity – generational, cultural, even gender perspectives.
- Leadership feedback, perceptions within the business.
- Social media interfaces and the use of various platforms.
- Technology awareness, e.g. apps for smart phones.

Of course, reverse mentoring is rarely one-sided. Senior staff could have decades of management experience and they have learned valuable lessons, including how to handle people and different situations. Most tacit knowledge is 'unGoogle-able', hence such insights may provide greater discernment than any social platform.

Mentoring relationships thrive on trust, respect and candour, but of course, too much candour can backfire if the new mentor crosses the lines of professionalism. Both parties need to have a healthy dose of emotional intelligence, which is vital to be able to gauge what's appropriate and what's not.

Perhaps we should start to challenge the thinking that, "Theirs is the belief that if you're senior, you have a lot to teach, and if you're junior, you have a lot to learn". We all have something to share, regardless of career level, which is why we must encourage others to define it and bring it to the table with positivity.

Formal vs informal mentoring

Informal mentoring (mentoring relationships that naturally evolve and develop) has contributed over the years in a significant way to the development of individuals in families, schools, communities, church groups and organisations. However, it has failed to provide concrete evidence of its value and the measurement of informal mentoring has notably been questioned. It has unfortunately not kept up with the trends in modern business, where the belief is that you "can only manage what you measure".

Mentoring has therefore evolved to become a more structured strategic business initiative and institutions are more than ever expecting to see a "return on relationship". It is for this reason that organisations have been tempted to structure and formalise mentoring.

We should recognise that formal/structured mentoring really grew from observing the unquestionable benefits that resulted from those first authentic mentoring relationships, which were the result of a natural affinity between two individuals.

Mentoring today is a vehicle to advance diversity, include minorities, and/or address demographic imbalances. The lack of diversity in most professions also created an opportunity to address these imbalances at the management level.

Mentoring provides career development opportunities, improved professional relationships, greater cultural understanding and inter-generational learning. Mentoring further offers opportunities to explore innovative ways to cope with the changing world of work and to be more adaptable to the constraints and challenges of the immediate environment. In an environment where change is the only constant, mentoring plays a critical role by supporting a transition, and encourages mentees to remain focussed on their own personal development.

The value-add of mentoring in business

- It is an authentic tool for both management and leadership development.
- It accelerates the competence, confidence and capacity of key role players in organisations.
- Ultimately mentoring harnesses the potential and strengths of employees to fully engage in their work environment.
- It promotes succession planning and skills transfer.
- Mentoring makes it simpler for employees to plot their career progression options. A better understanding of what is necessary to move up the career ladder or exposure to other functions provides multiple career options that make it more compelling to stay.
- It is a management tool for greater employee retention and engagement.
- It fosters a culture of learning in organisations.
- It accelerates more inclusive career development opportunities.
- Mentoring helps employees feel more connected to the purpose and values of the organisation.

- Mentoring could play a significant role during the induction and orientation of new employees, and even managers, to various levels within the organisation.
- It enhances a company's pipeline of talent; developing a bench of talent ensures greater sustainability for an organisation.
- It supports and reinforces the application of training and/or other educational interventions.
- It contributes to improved business performance.

The challenges of structured or formal mentoring

Formal or structured mentoring incorporates specific guidelines and structure to a mentoring relationship. The relationship lasts a predetermined or contracted period of time (usually from 9 to 18 months) and is focused on specific organisational or development objectives.

This form of mentoring really grew from observing the unquestionable benefits that resulted from informal mentoring relationships – interactions that were the result of a natural affinity between two people. Here are some significant differences.

Structured/Formal mentoring	Informal mentoring
As a result of a strategic business objective of the organisation.	Indefinite goals, mostly a result of some agenda and/or mutual attraction of the mentor/mentee.
Matched relationship based on criteria or some form of selection process.	Mentoring relationship develops naturally.
Measurable outcomes.	Unknown outcomes. Informally defined.

Structured/Formal mentoring	Informal mentoring
Access for all who qualify.	No criteria for inclusion, i.e. needs based.
Mentoring engagements last 9 - 18 months.	Relationship has no definite period – some relationships continue for years.
Capacity building for mentors and mentees.	Relationships left without any structure or goals.
Direct organisational benefits.	Non-specific organisational benefits.

Formal mentoring offers a distinct advantage in that it is an effective professional development tool that allows for measurement. Despite this, questions keep emerging about the challenges of the more formal/structured process:

- Should mentoring be thought of as a central strategy involving people development rather than a mere tool for a select few in the business?
- Must mentoring be part of good management practices and is it a role that managers should be expected to fulfil?
- What does it take to be a successful mentor and how should a faculty of competent mentors be identified?
- How should mentors be prepared for this challenge?
- What factors should be considered to match mentors and mentees?
- How can ordinary business relationships that show potential be encouraged to turn into profitable mentoring relationships?
- How do you measure the success of such an initiative?

Let us briefly explore the challenges of the formal/structured approach. Some key questions will highlight the concerns that organisations, and those that implement formal mentoring, grapple with. They may also allow you as a mentor to reflect on your specific mentoring relationship.

What is the purpose of formal mentoring in your business?

This becomes the most important question to answer before any attempt at institutionalising mentoring can be made. For some organisations, mentoring is about ensuring competitiveness, sustainability and growth by fast tracking high potential employees for definite positions. Others employ mentoring as a vehicle to develop and retain a leadership pipeline for critical positions within their business. Some proactively invest in graduate development to ensure not only a more demographic reflection of society, but also to develop a bench of talented young individuals as their business expands and grows.

A concerning trend is that organisations are willing to chase numbers in mentoring at the expense of profitable relationships. Most organisations pursue the value of mentoring without clearly defining what it is they would like to achieve! This not only makes it difficult to measure the true impact, but relationships (mentors/mentees) are expected to "make it work" without the necessary structure or end in mind.

Who should be mentors?

Finding the right mentors is possibly the greatest challenge for organisations that are pursuing a more structured mentoring programme. Administrators of mentoring programmes will testify that they have tried just about everything to engage the heart and minds of subject matter experts and those in critical operational positions to fulfil a mentoring role. Imagine an organisation where nothing happens without support from the top, where a 'project code' is necessary to engage employees' energy and time, where timesheets and Critical Performance Areas (CPAs) become the means by which they are rewarded, and people development is not one of those! The most successful mentoring relationships developed seamlessly without any form of coercion, manipulation or incentive!

In Jack Welch's words, "You can't force managers to love and care for people. It must come from the heart! Mentors have a different gene". Welch described this gene as "a love to see people grow; they get a kick out of seeing people being promoted, they celebrate their people, and have a generosity of spirit. They are not afraid to have strong people around them and have an abundance mentality when it comes to sharing knowledge, experience and lessons from life".

For parents this might come more naturally, but insightful mentors understand that when they invest in their mentees, they help shape the future and contribute to the sustainability of their organisation.

The reality is… without a pool of competent and willing mentors, any formal mentoring initiative is doomed to fail.

How should you match mentors and mentees?

Many seasoned mentors believe that a structured approach is "artificial" and based on a formal agreement. In structured or formal mentoring, the two parties do not come together as a result of a relationship that has grown organically into that of mentor – mentee. In fact, the task of matching often falls into the hands of a programme administrator.

The sheer amount of time and effort it takes to ensure "meaningful matches", where both mentor and mentee are comfortable with the process, makes it difficult to satisfy all role players. Some matches may do more harm than good because of these forced marriages.

A mentor should have a natural affinity for their mentee. Mentoring is relational so besides their competence and/or experience, mentors also need to be authentic, empathetic, trustworthy and honest. Mentors need to show that they are willing and interested in investing time in their mentee's personal and professional growth. A mentor is someone who will speak truth and will not shy away from constructive criticism or a reality check, while at other times they will encourage and celebrate progress and achievements. A well-chosen mentor can provide all of those things and will speak up for their mentee at tables where they don't have a seat.

Mentees must understand that a healthy mentoring relationship rests, to a large extent, in their hands. Mentees who have defined their own goals and expectations may reap many benefits, thus they need to communicate them clearly, take ownership for their development, and be willing to seek information about how to be successful in learning from mentors. The mentoring relationship should also be a priority for the mentee.

Unfortunately, the above qualities are prerequisites for profitable mentoring relationships and can never accurately be predicted nor authentically manufactured in a matching process. More often than not, when these qualities are absent, both mentors and mentees find their meetings awkward and even stressful as a result of this 'forced' intimacy. Predictably, involvement tends to peter out and the so-called mentoring relationship is degraded to nothing more than a 'now and then' coffee session.

Does the success of formal mentoring depend on the mentee?

Mentoring should also be embraced as a vehicle for personal development by those benefiting from it; mentees should show that they want to learn and demonstrate 'character' in order to maximise a relationship that could potentially make a significant impact in and on their lives and careers. Yet for mentoring to be 'profitable', the relationship needs to be characterised by common ground, high levels of trust, and openness that is reciprocal over time.

A profitable mentoring relationship differentiates itself from other working relationships in its level of intimacy as it deals with a number of crucial conversations and fairly sensitive topics, such as managing relationships, social graces, negotiating the company's political landscape, and personal growth and feedback. The above is, in my view, the responsibility of both the mentor and mentee.

The question remains: 'Does a formal mentoring programme/relationship create expectations that dampen the eagerness and hunger of the mentee?' 'Natural' or informal relationships evolve because both parties see something in the other and then seamlessly pursue the value of that which lies at the heart of the relationship, be it professional supervision, career advice, networking opportunities or greater business exposure.

How do you sustain a formal mentoring relationship?

The reality is that formal mentoring relationships need support to help prolong the relationship, but more so to ensure that the benefits of the mentoring relationship are met. This is the true challenge, as organisations are only willing to invest in such an initiative if there is a "return on relationship".

This in itself is a challenge, but more so when the culture in the organisation contradicts the value of people development. It is when operational efficiencies, business excellence, profit margins and bottom line results take priority to/over everything else, that mentoring relationships suffer the most!

Sustaining a mentoring relationship does require some form of structure, a healthy dose of good old discipline, and some input for conversations. These conversations should be to gain a greater understanding of purpose and goals, and to explore career aspirations. Mentors need to intentionally create opportunities to make sense of and discuss their mentees' performance. There should also be opportunities to highlight strengths and development areas, as well as conversations and exchanges on what is required to be successful, how to manage different relationships, and how to explore networks and build alliances. All of these 'crucial mentoring conversations' ultimately give the mentoring relationship a lot more to talk about — and possibly an opportunity to take action!

How much structure is necessary?

Besides contracting and agreeing on how to make their relationship meaningful, a mentor and their mentee could potentially find great benefit from a framework or some structure to facilitate some of these mentoring conversations.

To preserve a formal mentoring relationship it may be necessary to provide templates and guidelines, and to review meeting support. My corporate endeavours highlighted the challenge of this dichotomy. The structure that is provided to assist relationship A becomes the reason why it dampens the spontaneity in relationship B. This will not only differ from relationship to relationship, but also from organisation to organisation. The outcomes of the programme must dictate and the unique culture of the business should guide how much structure would be sufficient without overloading the relationship.

Clearly, structured mentoring relationships are exposed to a number of individual, interpersonal, and organisational challenges. Many formal programmes are costly, time consuming and simply do not reach enough employees.

These factors loom large in any mentoring relationship, and it is for this reason that I believe that it is important to highlight these realities right at the start of the book. It is furthermore critical to build the capacity of both mentors and mentees to maximise and leverage learning within a structured mentoring environment.

Despite these challenges, I have witnessed scores of structured mentoring relationships that have presented phenomenal growth results. Mentees will testify that they have been products of such mentoring relationships and here is the true value… the best way to reward a mentor is to become one for others. When formal relationships work they contribute to a culture where people informally pursue the value of mentoring as a development tool. Mentors publicly proclaim the importance of mentoring and the benefits they themselves gained from such relationships. In this way, they encourage others to experience the pleasure of seeing mentees develop, grow and ultimately succeed (whether formally or informally, short or long term, or as a result of a single action or an agreed-upon development plan).

The success of a structured mentoring relationship, like any other, depends on both parties' commitment to meeting the challenges of the relationship and taking full advantage of the opportunities that are presented – all of this with a clear end in mind for the relationship! This necessitates an intentional relationship characterised by purposeful discussions; deliberate, planned exposure; and well-intended pre-meditated actions.

The need to be more intentional as mentors

Parents, teachers, line managers and even business executives have an innate need to give back, sharing their own life stories, lessons learnt and what is required to be successful; they want to see others grow and achieve success. Most mentoring efforts fall short because of a lack of patience for time consuming or difficult processes. If you can ensure that participation in mentoring is quick and easy, it is not surprising to find that even executives will be more than happy to share their hard-gained experience and institutional wisdom.

To release the true value-add of mentoring, both mentors and mentees should grasp that their relationship might require less formality, yet enough intention/structure. It requires mentors to be deliberate in the opportunities to grow, develop, invest and build, while mentees need to actively pursue their relationship with one or more than one mentor.

Nurturing a profitable relationship

A profitable mentorship relationship is an association that is rewarding for both parties, and consists of meaningful and valuable discussions. Not only do these discussions add value to challenges and problem solving, but they also provide noticeable and significant contributions towards learning and the growth and development of the mentee. A profitable relationship is characterised by common ground, high levels of trust and openness, substance in discussions, and reciprocal outcomes over time for both parties.

This collaborative mentoring approach is rooted in the above principles, where a mentor and mentee achieve specific, mutually defined goals that focus on the development of the mentee's skills, competencies and thinking. The mentee plays an active role in the learning, ultimately becoming self-directed in the process. The mentor facilitates the mentee's capacity building over the course of the relationship.

What are these outcomes of mentoring? For a mentee, the benefits are enhanced promotion opportunities, greater confidence and competence in dealing with various personal and professional matters, greater employability and career mobility (to be discussed later in the conversation on career momentum), added professional competence, enhanced acceptance within and alignment to the organisation, and of course, most likely, a higher salary.

The benefits for the mentor are personal satisfaction and fulfilment, enhanced professional career identity, personal renewal and development, and recognition by the organisation and followers for developing talent. Possibly one of the greatest benefits that you could have as a mentor is the pleasure associated with shaping future generations!

The formation of the relationship

As previously noted, informal mentoring relationships (those that develop spontaneously, without a formal assignment or some matching process) are evaluated by both mentors and mentees as being more 'authentic' than formal (assigned) relationships. Mentees in informal relationships report greater effect from, and satisfaction with, a mentoring relationship that was mutually agreed to.

It appears that formally assigned mentoring relationships result in less rapport/connection, less relational comfort, less motivation and time for mentoring, and ultimately less communication and interaction. Most agree that the profitable mentoring relationships are based on common contributors to relational attraction, e.g. shared interests, trust, respect for diversity, frequent contact, and enjoyment of interactions. Finally, the most successful mentoring relationships are characterised by shared goals and expectations.

The above confirms that before getting involved in such a 'formal' process, mentors should carefully consider the intention of a mentoring relationship. The question, 'Why are we as an organisation involved in a mentorship endeavour?', and more specifically, 'What is the intention of my involvement in this relationship?', ensures that mentors are not just incidentally involved.

Mentees want to hear why their mentor is willing to be their mentor and why he said yes if asked or even appointed to the role.

For mentees, intentional mentoring means a form of open, social and collaborative learning. When mentees are intentional their learning is driven by their development needs, i.e. the learning is self-directed. When mentees are intentional they seek the right learning connections at the right time based on specific needs at that moment.

Intentional mentoring allows relationships to explore and learn moment by moment; it puts together mentors and mentees at the right time for the right purpose and for the right conversations, to find the right solutions for both personal and professional problems.

Intentional mentors ensure that their mentees become "definitively competent"

(*Extract from *Fundamentals for effective mentoring: Raising giant killers*)

"A mentorship relationship should be well planned (intentional) around development. Mentors should invest time and energy in getting to know their mentees, increasingly ensuring independence through confidence building, even carefully considering the ending of the relationship. Mentors should also intermittently evaluate how profitable the relationship is and if it provides value".

There are several definite yet interlinked focus areas where mentors could contribute to the complete or holistic development of their mentees.

Mentors could contribute to both the technical and professional competence of their mentees

Employees are expected to be 'hands-on' and competent in what they do. Operational requirements normally dictate this level and degree of (let's call it) functional or 'technical' competence. These key requirements for a mentee to function in his work might relate to knowledge, skill and experience. Functional or technical competence is normally the responsibility of the line manager or coach and is extremely job-specific, such as how to use a specific computer application, draft a contract, prepare a budget, execute a deal, or make a business presentation.

Mentors should also further encourage their mentees to become professionally competent. This will require mentees to develop expertise that will broaden their résumé of skills. Such skills professionally enhance their ability to deliver a product or provide a service with better quality, more efficiently. An example could be a great facilitator who might be technically competent, but does not know how to use certain technology that could enhance the delivery of a workshop. An attorney could be technically brilliant in a certain topic of the law, but would benefit professionally from a speed-reading course. A sales manager might be technically competent because of his knowledge of a product and the market, but lack professional competence as he is not conversant in English. Mentees who reject such opportunities may become occupationally marginalised and vulnerable when organisations retrench, change business focus or seek innovation.

Seasoned mentors understand the importance of migrating their mentees' skills from being technically competent to professionally competent!

Mentors should inspire and influence the appropriate "mindset"

Certain mentees are technically brilliant and competent, but cannot guarantee consistent results, especially when a significant outcome needs to be achieved. Mentors understand that their mentees might have unrealistic expectations that could impede their motivation and work performance. Mentees often get side-tracked because of work disappointments, business uncertainty, perceptions of unfair treatment, a tough line-manager, or conflict within peer relationships.

Mentors, therefore, need to challenge their mentees' thinking and encourage a positive mindset. Mentors need to teach their mentees to confront and solve, rather than to avoid or run away from, issues. It is vital for mentees to be perceived as value-adding individuals who operate with confidence despite previous setbacks, failures or disappointments. Experienced mentors will confirm that they have invested extensive time in this element, ultimately contributing to their mentees' enlightened and progressive mindset.

Mentors must reveal the need for institutional alignment

Workplace guidance enhances a mentee's sense of competence, identity, and work-role effectiveness. A mentee's road to success will be lined with stumbling blocks, difficult relationships and organisational bureaucracy and politics. Mentors have achieved success in the organisation and are for that reason more familiar with the realities of the organisation, its politics and its unique culture or way of doing things. This 'learning the ropes' will also include aspects that enhance and prepare mentees for advancement, sponsorship, exposure and visibility, as well as the provision of challenging assignments. In some organisations, the code of professional conduct may be unspoken and even the most talented mentee could be blind to the way things are done, while in others, the code may be quite overt. Mentees cannot afford to "push on doors that say 'pull'"; they need to understand how to get things done in and through the organisation, they need to understand the subtleties of the culture, and they need to know how decisions are made and how senior people think and operate.

This alignment between the organisation and the individual should be managed with sophistication. Mentors have a responsibility to share their wisdom in terms of unacceptable behaviours within the business, as well as the norms that set an acceptable range of behaviours. Ultimately, it is about teaching the mentees strategies to manage relationships in their areas of work, school, church, or business.

Mentors should convey the 'territorial wisdom'

Mentoring in the 21st century is indeed challenging. The complexities of our world, continuous innovations that bring about change, disruptive technologies, leadership challenges and even global trends, all create opportunities to discuss and learn. This means that mentors have to become deeply knowledgeable about the problems and issues of the day, and do whatever they can to contribute not only to finding solutions, but also to act responsibly. Mentors do not have to be accurate in their predictions, but rather convey the big picture of what is happening within and outside the world of their mentee. Mentees need to understand the conditions and complexities of their environment. The organisational trends, opportunities and threats that the organisation may face, and a better understanding of the customer as well as the competition, are all vital elements in contributing to a mentee's territorial wisdom. Mentors might create opportunities together with their mentees to assess the business landscape. Economic factors such as reviewing the company's or a competitor's business results, or even newsworthy events, can create opportunities to reflect, interpret and learn.

Mentors should help encourage their mentees to focus

Mentees cannot be definitively competent if they have not learned how to focus on their work, on the goals they have, on their development, and on their key priorities.

Focus relates to three levels:

- Learn to be more **conscious**. George Adams confirmed the importance of consciousness when he said, "There can be no advancement or success without serious thought". Consciousness is comparable to constant, unbroken thinking about an action, situation, event or undertaking, and implies a level of awareness of what needs to happen. Consciousness precedes the experience. When we worry about a situation or problem we allow ourselves to be conscious, possibly in a negative way. We need to learn to operate in the same way and apply "constant, unbroken thinking" when it comes to working on solutions, writing a book, taking the next step of a project, preparing a speech, or dealing with an important client. Being conscious and present helps mentees to prepare, to clarify choices, to consider decisions and to commit to actions.

- **Engagement** is all about paying attention to what is happening while so much is happening around us. If consciousness precedes the experience, then engagement is for the duration of, or during, the experience. Having a clear focus on the goal while we are busy with so many other priorities is critical. Engagement is potentially an area that mentees battle with in a mentoring relationship; they are so busy with their day-to-day functions that there seems to be no time for a mentoring relationship. Mentors need to assist their mentees to be more engaged when it comes to taking the initiative for a mentoring relationship, for example attending meetings, taking on assignments or projects, and taking steps to actionable outcomes.

- **Execution** is all about completing and finishing what was started. One of the greatest disabilities in organisations today is a culture that condones a lack of completion. Often people are good at talking, but poor at execution; workshops and sessions tend to be 'talk-shops'. Reflect on the actions from a previous work session or strategic meeting that have still not been executed. Mentees need to understand that execution is central to their success.

Skilful mentors seamlessly blend these focus areas in their relationship with their mentee and their development needs.

Being intentional about the 70-20-10

None of us will dispute the value of our education. When we exited school or a tertiary institution that provided wonderful opportunities, we would probably have called ourselves book smart. There is no doubt that education provides a solid foundation. If we recall, what was desperately lacking was being street smart or experience smart. The reality is that some skills and knowledge cannot be taught from a book. Despite this truth, most organisations follow a classroom model where a trainer presents information. A more modern approach is where some organisations employ e-learning to facilitate learning. Often these ways of training fall short of empowering delegates to put concepts into practice; they might even fail to provide the tools to apply the knowledge in the workplace.

Researchers at the Centre for Creative Leadership developed a model of learning in the mid-1980s which revealed that 70% of what people learn is through experience, 20% by means of exposure to the right people (mentoring, coaching and feedback), and only 10% is through education and training.

If we critically apply this thinking, we could safely say that organisations spend the majority of their money on education and formal learning, which constitutes only 10% of the learning spectrum. There is not nearly enough emphasis on how the 20% (mentoring, coaching and feedback) could facilitate/leverage greater experience in the 70% learning spectrum (job rotation, assignments/projects, on-the-job exposure).

Here is how intentional mentoring could be an underlying principle to enhance learning activities and ensure a more holistic development blueprint.

Provide blended learning to increase the impact of formal learning

There is a much greater ROI on formal training when relationships are established to connect mentees with mentors and coaches, before, during and after training. This allow participants with an opportunity to 'blend' course outcomes with on-the-job implementation. It also provides opportunities for mentors to support or connect the learner with other subject matter experts, ultimately expanding learning activities beyond the course.

Create collaborative learning environments

Modern mentors will encourage their mentees to network and build alliances with other individuals in and outside of their work environment. Such collaborative learning environments allow people to come together and learn from one another's work experience, sharing information and knowledge. Keith Ferrazzi's latest book, *Who's got your back*, confirms the reality that relationships are the key to success in business. Mentors must encourage their mentees to nurture the kinds of relationships that really make a difference in business. Ferrazzi stated that, "The real path to success in your career and in your personal life is through creating an inner circle of 'lifeline relationships' – close relationships with a few key trusted individuals who will offer the experience, encouragement, feedback, and generous mutual support that every one of us needs to reach our full potential". Whether your dream is to lead a company, be a top producer in your field, overcome the self-destructive habits that hold you back, lose weight, or make a difference in the larger world, nurturing such collaborative relationships is imperative for mentees.

Leveraging intentional mentoring

I recall my most valuable learning experiences, which have all been when I have had the opportunity to be part of a small group or project team for the sole purpose of brainstorming, sharing ideas, discussing trends or problem-solving. Mentors need to think less training and conferences and more exposure and on-the-job learning. The bulk of learning happens through observation and hands on experience; you don't learn how to swim by sitting next to a pool reading a book on swimming. Intentional mentoring provides opportunities for learning, but also captures and shares when mentees learn on the job.

A mentor recently shared a commitment she made to her mentee, which was to share a single e-mail a day – something from her inbox that she believes will benefit her mentee. It might be "for your attention", it could be "please read so that we can discuss at our next meeting", or "can I get your inputs on how we should respond to this". Intentional means 'planned', 'purposeful' and 'deliberate'.

Citing the above example, it is clear that mentoring is about building confidence. Intentional mentors are opportunistic and will seek out learning opportunities wherever they can. This does not mean that they take the responsibility for their mentees' development, but they show an understanding of, and a commitment to, their mentees' development needs. They could be valuable sounding boards during challenging assignments or high stake projects. They could also make themselves available to attend or observe, allowing more accurate feedback for their mentees. Intentional mentors will not hesitate to connect or exploit their own network to help their mentees.

Mentors also add value to their mentees by reflecting on their growth as well as their development journey. Crucial mentoring conversations provide an enhanced framework that allows mentors and their mentees to reflect on specific elements of a mentee's development journey.

Learning is a reflective process rather than some isolated event, and mentors must exploit that fully!

Part 2
An introduction to crucial mentoring conversations

A personal experience

I remember sitting at my desk at our corporate office in 1994. At 28, I was one of the youngest managers to be selected in my newly appointed role. I revelled at this achievement and my peers envied this opportunity. It allowed me to work on a project that granted me carte blanche and access to key stakeholders in the organisation. Add to that the benefit of a company car, a good salary and the autonomy I desperately desired, and I believed I was pretty much on the road to achieving my career goals and ambitions. David Lamola, a Senior General Manager in our business and informal mentor, walked into my office to congratulate me on the promotion. He was head of one of our operations and had a project-related query. A few minutes later our discussion evolved and he enquired about my age, qualifications and future plans. He then said something I will never forget. *"You know Niël, I am very glad for you. It is a great opportunity and you will gain good exposure. But this project will be done in 14 months and it will only prepare you for similar projects in the future. At your age, in my view, you should first be a good generalist before you become a specialist. Here you sit at HQ knowing more and more about less and less. Eventually knowing everything about nothing.* (He smiled). *Future opportunities inside and even outside of this business will require you to have more comprehensive exposure and bandwidth for you to move to the next level. I personally just feel uncomfortable that this is not what you need at 28."*

He then asked me to think about what I would like to write on my résumé 24 months down the line. *"Maybe that will give you a hint whether you are on the right track."* He then looked on his watch, said goodbye and left before I could respond. I sat there and stared at the door where he had just walked out on me. I had had one of my first crucial conversations; a conversation that shaped my career. Today I look at that conversation and recognise the profound impact it had on me and how it altered my decisions, actions and eventually my future.

All of us have engaged in one way or the other in similar conversations and experienced varying results. Some conversations leave us overwhelmed, anxious, disappointed and angry. Possibly even belittled. Other leave us with a promise, greater clarity, excitement and with a boost in confidence. When we engage in mentoring conversations we would obviously want to achieve the latter.

Demystifying crucial mentoring conversations

Communication and collaboration are central to the success of a mentoring relationship. Through it, mutual understanding emerges, common ground is developed, and ideas come to life. In short, discovery, understanding and learning happens in mentoring relationships through conversations. To enhance such an intentional effort, both mentors and mentees should be committed to productive, actionable conversations, i.e. crucial mentoring conversations.

Mentors in particular can play a significant role in encouraging conversations where they first get to know their mentees and learn from one another's personal experiences. Most mentors are conditioned to tell others how to proceed or fix a problem, but in mentoring relationships the intent should be to process results and help others discover the answers, rather than just to provide the solution. This will enhance the probability that the relationship will generate new awareness and insights and a higher level of understanding and experience. These conversations will ultimately impact the mentee's personal and professional development in a meaningful way.

A crucial mentoring conversation is not:

- a confrontational discussion;
- about picking the right time for dealing with a tricky topic;
- an attempt to create an opportunity to deal with robust feedback;
- concerning what is right or wrong; and
- about fixing a specific behaviour.

A crucial mentoring conversation is a discussion between a mentor and mentee (in some cases they intentionally involve other role players) that will assist both parties to break through to new levels of understanding and insight on specific topics. The mentee might find these conversations useful in both his personal and professional development. These conversations will trigger certain commitments and actions that will allow both parties to act because they have:

- greater clarity on a particular issue or topic, for example a mentee understands what behaviour inhibits productive relationships with colleagues and commits to specific actions;
- different perspective and views, for example a mentee understands how his performance on the job impacts his personal brand and how others see him in the organisation. He identifies specific actionable steps to deal with the matter; and
- more confidence to act on specific issues, for example a mentee discovers the value of various mentoring networks and sponsors and invests in specific opportunities to build those relationships and alliances.

The purpose of a crucial mentoring conversation

For the mentor:

Firstly, a crucial mentoring conversation provides greater context, clarity and an in-depth understanding of the specific issues or challenges the mentee faces. Asking the right questions not only provides context, but they also provide insight and opportunities that will facilitate problem solving.

Secondly, these mentoring conversations might allow for sharing of different perspectives, honest feedback, advice and recommendations, but in all of this it amplifies a greater appreciation and intimate understanding of the mentee.

Thirdly, a crucial mentoring conversation permits the mentor to share his own experiences, wisdom and insight on a specific topic or conversation.

A mentor needs to put himself out there to create a genuine and real connection with their mentee. Sharing personal stories will be one of the most powerful ways that a mentee can learn, relate and connect. Personal stories about the people, events and lessons that have shaped you makes you an authentic mentor; they speak about your values, your beliefs and what drives you as person.

Fourthly, these conversations will most certainly deepen your relationship with your mentee. It dramatically shortens the time it takes for a mentor and mentee to get to know each other at a completely different level. Mentors reap great satisfaction and fulfilment when they contribute to the personal and professional development of others.

Lastly, these crucial mentoring conversations broaden the true value-add of the mentoring experience.

For the mentee:

Imagine that a mentor could eliminate oversight with hindsight, foresight and insight. It would allow the mentee to explore and learn from their mistakes, to anticipate the advantages and disadvantages of a decision before they make it, and therefore to respond better in the moment. That is called wisdom!

A crucial mentoring conversation enables the mentee to **gain advantage from hindsight**. This is the knowledge and understanding gained from an event only after it has happened. The reality is that we often recognise the mistake only after we have made it! It is the recognition of the realities and the learning from moments that allow the mentee to deal with future matters in a more proactive or mature way.

A crucial mentoring conversation grants the mentee an opportunity to **acquire foresight**. It is the ability of imagining or anticipating what might happen in the future or might be required to be successful.

> Foresight is critical thinking concerning future conditions, responsibilities and commitments. Imagine the ability to perceive the advantages and disadvantages of a decision before it is made to avoid a mistake altogether.
>
> The conversations allow the mentee **greater insight**. It is the ability to interpret and respond in the present moment. It is that deeper understanding of a specific cause and effect in a given context – possibly a greater appreciation of an issue or another viewpoint, topic or situation. Practicing insight involves asking questions such as, "Is it a good idea to do this or not?" and "What would be the wise thing to do in this particular situation?"

Ingredients of successful crucial mentoring conversations

To ensure that participants leave a crucial being more productive and engaged, with a positive mindset and greater wisdom, the conversation needs four critical elements:

- Turn down the noise.
- Reciprocal contributions from both parties.
- Authentic trust in each other and in the purpose of the relationship.
- Action the abundant possible outcomes/assignments that come to light through these conversations.

• Turn down the noise

Mentoring should provide opportunities for a mentee to get to know himself better. We live in times of tremendous 'noise' and distraction, which are characterised by a breakneck pace of events throughout a calendar year, and most of us are guilty of filling schedules from early morning until late at night. We are desperately trying to keep up with the flood of information that pours through our laptops, mobiles and tablets, and instantly respond to the newest e-mail, the vibration of the latest

WhatsApp, the alert from our twitter feed or a new Facebook notification. Being connected to these technologies offers massive benefits, but inevitably draw our attention to the world around us. It encourages rapid responses and connectedness that forces us to reply often at some unreasonable times. We never get time to switch off… we hardly get time for ourselves, for opportunities for self-reflection and introspection. How about an electronic detox on occasion?

I know this is the 21st century, but I am convinced that smart technology will alter our worlds even more. It will also stimulate and enhance conversations on various topics. Just recently our family reflected on what we believe was the best animation movie of all time. A quick 'Google' on the topic "highest grossing animations" and soon we were yakking about our favourite characters and special moments.

Polly Berends wrote that, "Everything that happens to you is your teacher. The secret is to learn to step back from your own life and to then learn from it". Research supports this: one of the best ways to learn is through critical self-reflection and moments to capture the learning.

Mentees often complain that they could not find the time to spend with their mentors, so they need to reflect where and when they can turn down the noise – to journal their experiences, insights and learnings. By no means do I suggest lengthy 'Dear diary' entries. In a mentoring context, I would suggest to mentees a series of weekly informal, private notes, the purpose being to ensure that the learning does not stop at the end of the mentoring session, the class work or project meeting. For example:

- What did I find most difficult to deal with this month?
- What part of the project work did I enjoy most?
- Which relationship at work do I find the most draining and why?
- What have I discovered about my own ability to work under pressure and to meet deadlines?

Journaling compels us to access our memories of an experience, and to reflect on the learning, the emotions and insights. The aim is to go beyond the daily noise in our mind and the endless agenda of tasks and daily priorities that do not offer self-reflection.

Most importantly, these insights allow for opportunities to connect in our mentoring relationships – often leading to crucial mentoring conversations.

- **Reciprocal contributions from both parties**

Mentors need to ensure that both parties are committed to the relationship and contribute in a spontaneous way. Reciprocal does not mean a forum for true confessions, but rather a concerted effort to share information and transfer knowledge bilaterally within the relationship. We have discussed the value and richness of reverse mentoring. The younger generations are comfortable with a reciprocal mentoring relationship in which they share their accumulated knowledge to teach others. Millennials do more than consume information: they respond, exchange, recommend, share, and criticise where necessary. Expect them to be honest in their own evaluation of your role and contribution as mentor.

Conversations tend to be less productive when:

- there is too much telling. The individual can come across as being disinterested in the opinions and views of others. They create the impression that they know it all, causing resentment and polarisation;
- there is too little telling. The person can seem cold and aloof, not showing interest in the conversation on relationship. This could create a relationship that does not encourage openness and that does not feel warm or sincere; and
- there is too much questioning/asking. The person can appear to be the interrogator with the sheer purpose of gathering information, without the willingness to openly share themselves. This could potentially lead to suspicion or even a lack of trust.

- **Authentic trust in each other and in the purpose of the relationship**

Steven R. Covey said, "Trust is the glue of life. It is the most essential ingredient in effective communication. It is the foundational principle that holds all relationships". According to his son, Stephen M. R. Covey, author of *The Speed of Trust*, low trust causes friction and creates agendas, interpersonal conflict, win-lose thinking, and defensive and protective communication. On the other hand, Covey maintained that if trust is developed and leveraged, it is the one thing that will create unparalleled success, and is also key to successful mentoring relationships.

The level of trust is influenced by the quality of the connection, yet the quality of the connection between mentor and mentee is also influenced by the level of trust. No matter which way you look at it, trust is without a doubt the cornerstone to crucial mentoring conversations and ultimately profitable relationships. Trust is the glue that holds relationships, families, communities and organisations together.

What does it mean when you say you trust someone?

After more than 10 years of research that included focus groups with CEOs, managers, teachers, parents and associates, I am now convinced that trust is something that grows when certain behaviour is present. Let us say that trust is based or influenced though behaviour. In my experiments, I set up flipcharts during sessions where delegates could document their views on what behaviour builds trust or breaks/erodes trust.

People came up with an assortment of answers. For some it was hard to trust – they felt that people had to 'earn' their trust by exhibiting certain behaviours. The fact that they could trust was based on the performance of an individual on aspects such as being reliable or on time. In their view, individuals who would deliver on their promises and do what they said they would do could be trusted. Trust was even based on the competence of the individual, or the fact that they could be counted on when the going got tough. Modelling integrity and exhibiting consistency and dependability were often mentioned.

For another group of participants, there needed to be a much deeper emotional connection before they said they could trust. These individuals placed a premium on the sincerity of the individual and feeling valued and respected. Trust was imbedded in how they were treated. For them, trust is that safe place where they were allowed to have some say in a relationship that allowed them to share without fear of getting lectured or judged; they wanted to be listened to and understood.

It became evident that trust means different things for different people based on their experiences. This begged the question, 'How do we ever talk about or build trust if we see it only through our own lenses?' Clearly, we need a common framework that can create a mutual language for trust. Let's call it key trust elements.

The intent of this section of the book is to raise your awareness of the importance of trust and the specific behaviours that cultivate greater levels of trust in a mentoring, and for that matter any, relationship.

The 3 key promotors of trust

Surely the goal of mentoring is to provide guidance and support to an aspiring mentee? It takes time to establish a trusting relationship where both mentor and mentee can learn from each other and devise a development plan to reach the desired outcomes. It requires trust to work together and tackle the challenges that most aspiring mentees face, like overcoming fears, building confidence, and taking risks.

It can be tempting to equate the level of trust with the level of communication. This can be misleading. Some mentees might find it difficult to connect or find it challenging to share too much initially. Whether they show it or not, your mentee is looking for an outlet for their thoughts, experiences and feelings. As with any relationship, trust evolves slowly through the simple process of being together on a regular basis.

It is a mentor's responsibility to proactively and purposely inspire and cultivate trust. A high trust environment is one where the relationship can share, pull together and do what is necessary to overcome the challenges facing their situation or relationship.

In modern mentoring I believe there are three key promotors/cultivators of trust.

Competence

When mentors exhibit their skills or share their experiences from past accomplishments, it potentially validates their reputation of competence and the level of trust that others have in them. For trust to form, mentors will have to demonstrate their competence in any given area and the competence to share that expertise. These areas may include technical skills, certain qualifications and experiences, managerial skills, leadership and business knowledge, team management skills and dealing with people.

Behaviour that cements competence as a promoter of trust

- Clarify expectations and then **deliver on promises**.
- **Drive quality results**. Using your skills and committing to high standards of work will win the trust of others.
- **Be on time** and inside budget.
- **Share lessons** from personal insights and experiences.
- **Practice accountability**.
- **Be responsive** and follow up. When goals are set, it is vital to show a joint commitment and that you as a mentor are taking the process seriously.

Character

Those who do what they say they are going to do inspire trust. The same can be said of those who speak openly and honestly about their principles, beliefs and opinions. Integrity is demonstrated when behaviours and values are aligned by maintaining confidentiality, keeping your word, and ensuring that others feel that they can speak their minds without fear of depredation.

Behaviour that fortifies character as a cultivator of trust

- **Keep your word** means to take actions that fulfil promises made. Are your actions consistent with your words?
- **Be sincere.** Make sure that your words match the feelings in your heart. Pay honest compliments.
- **Encourage transparency** in all interactions.
- **Talk straight and be consistent.** Predictability is a good thing. When people know how strongly you feel about something and how you will respond rather than letting your moods dictate your behaviour, people come to know you as someone who can be trusted.
- **Lead by example.** Don't be judgemental of others and don't discuss any individual with your mentee. It will create an atmosphere of safety where your mentees won't feel they are being judged. Refusing to gossip is a rare habit worth cultivating!
- **Admit when you are wrong.** Be hasty to acknowledge oversights, wrong judgements and personal mistakes. Not only is it liberating, but it inhibits the malicious efforts of others. So, be critical of your own conduct and share your commitments to rectify matters.
- **Live your values.**

Caring

Mentors need to show concern for, and interest in, those they mentor. Mentors can exhibit this when they show interest in the expressed development needs and aspirations of their mentees. When mentors actively listen, they create a safe place where others can share professional concerns, personal difficulties, or an opportunity to raise topics that might not be appropriate to discuss with others. Encouragement is a vital role that mentors play to offer support, provide hope and build confidence.

Part 2: An introduction to crucial mentoring conversations

Behaviour that augments care as a cultivator of trust

- **Show respect** for others. Regardless of race, age, gender, culture, religion, status or position, others are worthy of respect. Extending respect without prejudice models behaviour that says everyone deserves to be valued and regarded.

- **Show genuine interest** in your mentee and display a spirit of generosity. The relationship is not about you.

- **Express encouragement** to pursue goals and to continue despite challenges or stumbling blocks. Encouragement is the act of stimulating the development of an activity. Encouragement and support are the two most recognised contributions that mentees appreciate in their mentors. **Remember, everyone needs a cheerleader!**

- **Listen to cultivate understanding/empathy** rather than to respond or give advice to solve problems. Showing a sensitivity for others' feelings and concerns opens the door to trust.

- **'Protect'** your mentee from harmful intentions, destructive interactions and negative connections.

- **Reinforce** your mentee's positive qualities/strengths, talents and behaviours. When mentors endorse these qualities and efforts, they demonstrate high expectations and trust in their mentees' abilities.

- **Share your own vulnerabilities,** not as a display of weakness, but as an effort to validate your own limitations. Others feel more at ease when they can relate and see the 'human' side of their mentor (this does not mean, and it is not recommended, that you need to share highly personal or private matters).

These promotors of trust are not some magic wand. Like anything in life, it requires practice and deliberate efforts. Mentors should focus on the impressions they make during these interactions. The promotors of trust may not transform your relationship overnight, but through greater awareness of preferences, cultures and differences, these engagements will contribute to more profitable mentoring relationships.

- **Resulting actions/assignments that come to light through these conversations**

The measure of a productive mentoring relationship is the resulting action that it produces. Conversation for the sake of conversation rarely leads to changed behaviour. Mentors and mentees should come to a specific agreement about what they would like to action from their different conversations. Who is going to do what by when? When actions flow from these conversations and follow ups ensure execution of commitments/promises, the relationship turns profitable.

Effective mentoring relationships build confidence and develop competence in both the mentee's personal and professional development areas. Action and execution will be discussed in more depth at the end of the crucial conversation section.

The topics that crucial mentoring conversations can/should cover

When you mentor intentionally, opportunities for crucial conversations present themselves repeatedly – they lie all around us, all the time – from 'What's my purpose?' to career challenges, performance appraisals, and navigating various relationships at work. The skills we need in the boardroom and in our personal lives are the same.

This book covers eight different crucial conversations that could offer breakthroughs in self-awareness and potentially add value to any mentoring relationship. They can be discussed based on the needs of the mentee in any particular order, or the requirements for success in a certain situation or environment, e.g. leadership requirements for a business. Some mentors use them merely as an informal framework to validate discussions they would like to have with their mentees.

Part 2: An introduction to crucial mentoring conversations

Figure 1: Crucial conversations

Who should own or drive these conversations?

The mentee should determine how long and how formal the relationship should be. When mentees acknowledge that their personal (e.g. family, religion) and professional lives (e.g. careers and networks) can be enhanced through a series of planned experiences and interactive conversations, they should determine the depth of support and guidance needed to achieve their goals.

Like an entrepreneur who exhibits qualities including an unwavering passion for what they do, open-mindedness to learn from others, the desire to be the best at what they do, and a forward-looking approach, mentees need to be entrepreneurial learners. What does this mean? John Seely Brown explains in his book, *Shift Happens*, that "The entrepreneurial learner is constantly looking for new ways, new resources, new peers and potential mentors to learn new things". Brown goes on to explain the concept. "An entrepreneurial learner interested in leadership will search websites dedicated to leadership. The websites for example, make no demands on its users; there are no tests or lectures, yet learning happens all the time. The learner will download what is for free and explore the richness of the topic by connecting and collaborating with others across the world. They will also use mentors to jointly create context and learning."

Learners who are ambitious, focused and motivated qualify as the best mentees. They pursue learning and take full responsibility for their own personal development. They value relationships and appreciate the value and time of those who share their tacit knowledge.

The role of the mentor in these crucial conversations can best be described as a 'guide'.

You will be presented with a framework of possible questions on each of the crucial mentoring conversations, as questions encourage learning by allowing your mentee to reflect. Questions that require thoughtful answers challenge, but also help, a mentee to articulate their own thinking on the topic that is explored.

Questions will engage your mentee in each crucial conversation. Remember that questions need to be appropriate to fit age, gender, culture and religion.

Please note the mentor's role is not a leading role; the ownership, initiative and accountability for the outcomes of the relationship rest heavily on the shoulders of the mentee.

When should you have a crucial conversation?

Mentors need to be aware of:

- what is happening in the life of their mentee;
- what the high-stakes moments and opportunities for learning are; and

- how they can clarify understanding or create a more in-depth context of the topic.

Intentional mentors will facilitate specific discussions at the appropriate time. They are opportunistic because they understand the application value of hindsight, foresight and insight. There is no better time to talk about safety than when the issue is highlighted and calls for learning, and no better time to talk about the importance of values when there is a great lesson to learn from.

Inevitably both mentors and mentees bring different levels of experience and needs to the relationship. Mentors should understand that with the development of any new skill, learning can be broken down into four stages:

- Unconsciously incompetent.
- Consciously incompetent.
- Consciously competent.
- Unconsciously competent.

Table 2: Four stages of learning

Stage	Learner response	Mentor contribution
Level 1 Unconscious incompetence	Learners are unaware of what they do not know. Confidence exceeds competence/ability.	Support discovery and encourage. Learning (blind spot awareness). Crucial mentoring conversation on performance – give feedback.

Stage	Learner response	Mentor contribution
Level 2 Conscious incompetence	Learners are now aware of what they don't know. Confidence evaporates with reality check.	Create understanding of gaps. Ask questions to deepen understanding and self-awareness. Crucial mentoring conversation on 'fitness' – give feedback.
Level 3 Conscious competence	Learners are hungry to learn more. They know the process and exhibit the necessary skills.	Encourage opportunities to practice. Validate abilities. Crucial mentoring conversation on 'strengths' – give feedback.
Level 4 Unconscious competence	Learners no longer think about what they are doing. High levels of confidence.	Reflect on abilities. Encourage continuous improvement or stretch to next level of challenges.

Mentors are also perceptive when the following questions arise:

- Is your mentee getting results that he doesn't want, e.g. he is unsuccessful in a job interview?
- Is he failing to get results that you would like to see, e.g. a poor presentation at a meeting?
- Does he have persistent, recurring problems, e.g. negative relationships?

- Is trust or respect diminishing, e.g. comments made by your mentee that flag issues that may need to be addressed?
- Is he doing what he really should be doing, e.g. has there been a sudden shift of focus or new interest that takes up the bulk of his time?
- Are there uncertainties about what he should be doing next, professionally, e.g. the mentee feels he is at a crossroads in his career?
- Are they really bugged/disturbed/distracted by something, e.g. a destructive relationship with a line-manager that impacts on their level of confidence?
- Are there high stake moments that require a conversation as preparation or an intervention, e.g. an important presentation to request budget for a project?

Creating success at having crucial mentoring conversations

This chapter provides a template for each conversation, which the mentor might find useful to facilitate the different discussions, but let us first explore the intention or purpose of the mentoring relationship and then the actual crucial mentoring conversation.

So often we have relationships just for the sake of having them. Regrettably, this leaves many mentoring relationships that do not provide value. It is important to know what you want out of a relationship. What are your motivations? Why are you willing to be a mentor? What value do you wish to give and receive? Do you want to control because of your status, position or role, or do you want to establish and maintain a relationship of trust and mutual cooperation?

Before entering a crucial conversation, we should also ask, "What do I really want for me?", "What do I really want for my mentee?", "What do I really want for our relationship?" If you want to get the most out of your relationship it is imperative that you have some sort of expectation of what you wish to give and receive from a particular conversation.

Mentors should lead a conversation with stories, observations and questions, as opposed to conclusions and emotions. When you use these tools, you start these conversations with your mentee from a place of safety and mutual purpose.

The power of storytelling… "A long time ago in a galaxy far, far away…"

I bet most of us will have fond memories, even emotional connotations, just reading the above caption.

Stories connect people in a profound way; storytelling is a natural form of communication and needs very little explanation. Stories strengthen cultures, enhance beliefs, and pass on wisdom from one generation to the next. Stories especially told face-to-face transmit these experiences, insights and lessons. These images, lessons or even metaphors will remain in the memory longer than any speech, sermon or lecture.

For mentors, it is a powerful way to guide a conversation, to convey a message, and even to inspire a mentee. It becomes an extremely powerful tool to build common ground through sharing narratives, giving accounts, and telling tales. Mentors must tell authentic, emotive and compelling stories that are interesting and capture the attention of the listener. Stories enhance a greater understanding of the topic or storyteller, supplementing appreciation and respect, and influencing views and dreams.

Perhaps the most interesting part of storytelling is that it has a great effect on our brains. Our brains release a chemical substance called dopamine when we experience an emotionally charged event. Dopamine allows us to remember our experience better and with greater accuracy. Think about it – we are wired to remember stories much more than data, facts, and figures. While a great story will be remembered for a long time, a boring fact will easily be forgotten. Stories stick!

When is storytelling powerful?

It is important to make sure that the story facilitates the actual mentoring conversation, the desired insight, and ultimately influences the possible action. The key is to select the type of story that will generate an intentional response from your mentoring partner.

When you have a story to tell about yourself

Example: "Can I tell you what the turning point in my career was…?"

These stories reveal something important about how you think and feel, and what motivates you. Using a personal example adds to your authenticity as a mentor and can speak volumes to those with whom you are building deep relationships.

When you want to share a particular lesson

Example: "I will never forget the most important lesson I have ever learned about leadership…"

These stories illustrate the amount of understanding that you have or how much you have gained over a given amount of time. It often helps to share the critical events and experiences that have contributed to your understanding, thus building credibility.

When you need to illustrate a moral or ethical issue

Example: "Can I tell you about the most difficult situation I faced, when my integrity was tested?"

These stories demonstrate life lessons using personal experiences or observations. Concepts like integrity, honesty, or servant leadership are often best conveyed using a moral tale or a personal story that illustrates the point.

When you want to communicate across boundaries (culture, gender, religion, generation)

Example: "Let me tell you a powerful metaphor from nature; in nature it is about survival of the fittest and those that are most adaptable…"

You can also use themed analogies involving sports, cooking, child rearing, etc. These stories provide opportunities for viewpoints and conversations that might have been difficult because of diversity in a mentoring relationship.

When you want to share a truth

Example: "I want to tell you what happened to me during my student years…"

Factual stories present a series of events or actions in an 'as-they-happened' style. These types of stories can be used to inspire reflective discussion, update progress, demonstrate understanding, or illustrate a point.

We now know that storytelling allows us to understand and connect with the world and those around us, and helps us feel like we are a part of something. It is a memorable and valuable social/development tool.

Three critical aspects of stories to remember

Make sure that all stories have a beginning, middle and end.

Beginnings orientate the listener to the story, the timeline and the setting, as well as introducing the main characters and scenario. The middle of the story is where you provide important details and developments, while the end shares the results, conclusions, and summary of the lesson learned.

Carmine Gallo writes in her book, *The Storyteller's Secret*, "Show me an inspiring leader and I will relate with you their story that influences the way they see the world. Storytelling is not a luxury, it's a necessity. We cannot imagine a world without it because the self is a story. If the self is a story, then we are all storytellers".

The ancient Greek philosopher Plato said, "Come then let us pass a leisure hour in storytelling and our story shall be the education of our future heroes". What he meant was that stories themselves create, inspire and guide others to live their own narratives.

Sometimes a good personal anecdote is the perfect way to make a point. Your mentee wants to learn from your experiences, after all. But don't start telling too many stories that are more indulgent of yourself than helpful to the mentee. Remember, this relationship is a two-way street, not a lecture hall.

What stories do you have that are worth telling?

Ensure honesty and safety in your conversations

People don't get defensive because of the *content* of what you're saying, they get defensive because of the *intent* they perceive behind it and how it is said. When others become defensive, stop talking about the issue and clarify the purpose of the conversation. Help them understand your motives by sharing what you really want from the conversation – for them and for the relationship.

When crucial conversations become intimidating the problem is not too much candour, it's too little safety. With enough safety, you can talk about anything.

It might be valuable to gain insight from other role players prior to certain conversations. It provides an opportunity to explore how others see the issues as you spend time sharing your own. *Exploring* means that you are genuinely curious about others' views. Your goal is not necessarily to agree with them, but instead to discover how a reasonable, rational and objective person would think and feel.

The sweet aroma of authenticity

When purchasing expensive perfume, you'll want to know that you're buying the real deal. Imitation perfumes are easily manufactured but don't have the same quality or scent as the authentic perfume, so you don't want to waste money on them. Understanding the 'signs' of fake perfume can help you make an informed choice. Here are a few steps that a potential buyer would complete to validate the authenticity of a perfume.

- The buyer will ideally try to meet the seller, normally not on some street corner but rather a department store.
- Research the perfume beforehand.
- The longevity of a scent depends on the amount of oils in the product.
- Check the price; if it is cheap it is too good to be true.
- A buyer will inspect the packaging and look at and feel the bottle, but it is probably in the smell that the real deal is revealed.
- The smell of genuine perfume will always last longer. The less diluted your scent is, the longer it lasts.

This analogy to perfume illustrates the importance of authenticity in relationships. A mentor's charm or attractiveness, like any relationship within a family, at school, in church, as leaders, will be tested for authenticity in a similar way. Our packaging, intentions, willingness, conduct, actions, and what we say and do is part of 'how we smell' and 'how long we last'. Mentors are scrutinised for authenticity, thus all aspects of your life need to 'smell authentic' to make yourself attractive to others.

How can mentors exhibit greater authenticity?

Share your story

We have previously discussed the power of storytelling. Make sure you have a clear understanding of your own personal journey. Each of us is a fusion of our own life experiences; when you own your own story you will better understand the wonderful rich moments that shaped your past. Authentic mentors frame their stories in ways that allow others to see themselves not as passive observers, but as individuals who learn from their own experiences. Mentors make time to reflect on their own experiences, and in doing so they grow as individuals and as leaders. Presenting yourself just the way you are is a powerful statement that includes a stamp of authenticity.

Practice what you preach

It's not about stating that you are authentic, it's about practicing what you preach, all the time and in every way. Does your behaviour match your promises and values?

The mentee you are mentoring looks up to you. He immediately vests responsibility in you as a mentor. Authenticity in your behaviour is key to maintaining this relationship. It can be as simple as being on time; if you emphasise the importance of delivering on time, but then are consistently 15 minutes late to meetings, that's not particularly authentic. It can even be about your reputation. If you have a public persona of being calm and constructive, but then throw temper tantrums to get the attention of your staff, how do you think that'll impact them? We all make mistakes, but when you do you need to own them, apologise, correct things, and move forward. As a mentor, this is especially important.

Get your own feedback

Authentic mentors also work hard at developing self-awareness through persistent and often courageous self-exploration. Denial can be the greatest hurdle that mentors face in becoming self-aware, but authentic mentors ask for, and listen to, honest feedback. They also use their own mentors and other formal and informal support networks to help them stay grounded and lead integrated lives. Mentors who benefit from other mentoring relationships, or even reverse mentoring, reveal their own development needs and even share their own vulnerabilities. Brene Brown explains in *The power of vulnerability* that, "we associate vulnerability with emotions we want to avoid such as fear, weaknesses and uncertainty. Yet we too often lose sight of the fact that vulnerability is also the birthplace of authenticity and acceptance. Vulnerability is, in truth, our most accurate measure of courage and saying who we are".

I think the most attractive mentors are those who reveal that they do not know everything; mentors who show that they are just human after all. The best way to practice vulnerability is to admit when you don't have the answer, to share what is making you lie awake at night, or to share the frustrations with the uncertainty of a project or the future.

Celebrate your own uniqueness

Joseph Campbell commented that, "The privilege of a lifetime is being who you are".

A key component of authenticity is simply knowing who you are and being comfortable with yourself. This requires taking the time to develop informed ideas about the things you care about, and not blindly adopting them from others around you. It is with this foundation that you are able to live those values – stand behind them, represent them and feel strongly about them.

Knowing yourself means you understand what you need. For myself, I:

- need to give. There is nothing that gives me greater pleasure than to know that I have made a contribution or given something – resources, time, advice – that others desperately needed;
- need to know that I am adding value. It is very much part of my purpose; as soon as I feel that I don't add value my energy diminishes;
- need to spend time marketing. It is the only way that I can ensure a pipeline of work for our business. It allows me to manage my levels of stress;
- need to be organised. I love to be in control, and considering the amount of traveling I do, it enables me to make my life as simple as possible;
- need to spend quality time with my wife and boys. It fills my tank – they love me, tease me and make me laugh;

- need just a few good friends who understand me, appreciate me and challenge me;
- need to exercise. It makes me feel good about myself and reminds me of the blessing of good health;
- need to get good rest. I cannot function properly without at least seven hours of uninterrupted sleep; and
- need to have quiet time. This is where I charge my batteries, and where I strengthen my faith and connect with God.

Do you understand your need list?

People who have really looked within to understand why they think and act the way they do are clearer about the principles – and purposes – that drive their lives. When we are comfortable with ourselves we can immerse ourselves in different perspectives. We need to know who we are, what we believe in and what we stand for. This makes mentors proactive, but also attractive.

Recognise the diversity in others

The quickest way to a 'non-profitable' relationship is to try to change the person with whom you have a relationship. Think about it, relationships aren't meant to clone or to force change. It is not your job as a mentor to change your mentee! You are there to help them grow, but how they grow is up to the person facing the path of growth. The only person you should want to change is yourself!

Many people, including parents, invest in relationships hoping to make a particular person or their children more like themselves – to influence their opinions and to change their habits. All these cloning efforts do, however, is create resentment, and blocks the relationship from reaching its fullest potential.

It's okay to not always agree. Relationships would be stale and boring if that was the case. Once you begin to appreciate the uniqueness of others you will soon begin to grow and even appreciate your own uniqueness more.

Straight talk will promote openness

If you wish to live a life rich with authentic relationships, it is an absolute must that you learn to talk straight. Mentors need to convey their message in a straightforward manner that can be easily understood; so often we load our communication with diplomacies to mask our true intentions.

If we have a problem with something, we should say it. When we hint we leave our thoughts and feelings up to interpretation. Be straightforward and honest. Remember that your point of view is simply that – your perspective; it doesn't mean you're right or wrong. A conversation about straight talk is vital. As much as there is a need for mentors to talk straight, mentees themselves should appreciate the value of honesty. Soul to soul communication can only occur when we consciously choose to put our shields down and allow ourselves to share and receive.

At what stage should confrontation be part of a crucial conversation?

It might be an option, even a necessity, to confront during a crucial mentoring conversation. 'Confront' has two meanings:

- To oppose, provoke or threaten.
- To be gentle, supportive and accurately reflect what you have observed.

The idea is to help your mentee to explore an issue deeply, with the goal being the formulation of a new idea or plan that will benefit them.

Leading indicators for confronting might be:

- when you sense potential risks or failures that might damage the reputation of your mentee;
- when you notice non-committed or unproductive behaviour;
- when your mentee is shifting responsibility or not recognising reality;

- when you want to draw focused attention to a specific issue; and
- when you doubt the ability of others to contribute or get results.

Consider the following:

Observe

If the opportunity is available, a mentor might observe a mentee, possibly in a presentation, during an interaction with peers and seniors, or when they are leading a meeting. While a mentor would want to be as unobtrusive as possible, direct observation can give a mentee tremendous insight from a respected ally. This will allow you, as a mentor, to cite specific instances when your mentee has given you cause for concern or validated specific feedback. The value of observation is so rich. You need to see how your mentee reacts in the heat of the moment, e.g. when he is squeezed to deliver on a tough deadline or when his budget is slashed to almost nothing.

Articulate

When openly voicing your disagreement or opposition to a mentoring partner, it is best to be as clear and direct as possible. Avoid attack, disapproval, or personal judgments. Stay solution-focused and positive about possible outcomes. It usually helps to clarify your position or reason for addressing the issue of concern at the onset of the conversation. When giving feedback, stick to what was seen or heard; avoid giving your impression of the mentee or what you have heard from others. If you don't do this, you risk raising suspicion or mistrust regarding your agenda or motives for the conversation. Doing so helps lessen the perceived judgment about the mentee.

Validate

To help the mentee process the feedback, start by linking it to a developmental goal or to some issue with which he is dealing. This step helps the mentee to see the bigger context before reacting to the feedback itself. When you confront, you need to be willing to listen to your mentee's reactions and help them process your observations and comments. While you should not take ownership of what they do with your advice, you have a responsibility to own the proper interpretation of your intent and meaning, and clarify yourself if needed.

The power of questioning

In general, confronting questions focus on clarifying intent and meaning behind behaviour.

Sample questions include:

- Have you noticed…?
- Can I share with you my observations on…?
- What do you think will be the implications of…?
- Are you aware that…?
- Are you willing to think differently about…?
- How does this align with your purpose, objectives, values?
- Can I correct your assumption regarding…?

Mentors require emotional maturity and sensitivity that allows them to sensibly, affectionately and with dedication confront their mentees in their mistakes. Mentors should themselves be open and even desire to have others confront them.

How to end a crucial mentoring conversation?

End with assessing a clear understanding; don't be satisfied with just a good talk. Come to a specific agreement about what the key take-away should be for the mentee, or even who is going to do what by when. If this is the case, then agree when to follow up to see that both of you have kept these commitments. Clear agreements and disciplined accountability turn great conversations into great results/actions.

The importance of action and execution

In order for mentoring to be effective, we need to engage in actionable conversations. Generating ideas or exploring alternatives with a trusted advisor are important and inspire high energy, but for mentoring relationships, this is just the beginning of meaningful conversation and a profitable relationship.

The measure of a crucial mentoring conversation is the resulting action that it produces. Effective mentoring increases ability, skill and confidence, with the ultimate goal of personal or professional transformation.

Conversation for the sake of conversation rarely leads to changed behaviour. In fact, crucial mentoring conversations that do not focus on actionable change give the illusion of transformation without delivering any actual change in behaviour. The end result is that your mentee embraces new concepts like 'servant leadership' or 'multiplying the talents of staff', but holds on to old behaviours by new names. In this way, it feels like the relationship is making progress when in reality you are simply changing the terminology.

Discussing concepts, ideas, and answering questions are all important and valuable aspects of dialogue, but for mentoring conversations to be 'profitable', there is a need to move beyond this to include intended and anticipated actions. Simply put, mentoring conversations need to conclude planned actions.

John Maxwell summed up this challenge in this way: "The key to becoming a more efficient leader/manager is not to check off all the items on your to do list every day. It's in forming the habit of prioritizing your energy and time so that you can accomplish your most important goals in an efficient manner".

Failure to shift conversation into action can lead to the following dysfunctions in the mentoring relationship:

- **Lack of commitment**. It's easy to engage in conversations without having a desire to do something different or improve performance. Mentors needs to show their commitment to a relationship as much as mentees do. It might be reading an article, preparing feedback on an assignment, arranging a follow up, or just making time for the next conversation that exhibits your loyalty to the mentoring process. Mentors should take note, remind and follow up on commitments made. When mentees observe the interest and commitment of their mentors they cannot avoid their own responsibilities or ignore the actions they need to take.

- **Lack of challenge**. When there is very little actionable feedback being discussed or new action being taken, the conversation stays at a high concept level and not enough personal information is shared. These conversations are easy to engage in, but they rarely create a personally challenging environment. Transformation seldom takes place when there is little personal challenge or responsibility to act. Mentors should challenge and stretch their mentees by confirming the high expectations they have.

- **Lack of measure**. This occurs when there is very little thought or consideration given to accomplishing new results. When nothing is measured, nothing is usually gained. If there is perceived gain, there is no way of determining if it was above or below expectations, because measurable results were never projected. Mentors should make an effort to remind their mentees just how much progress they have made or how much they have grown.

- **Lack of improvement**. When there is no measure, the mentoring relationship stays at a hypothetical or conceptual level. Mentoring conversations then tend to skip and meander across broad topics without concentrating on clear actions. In this case, when pressed on why the planned actions were not undertaken, you are likely to hear your mentee's excuses regarding poor timing, other commitments, lack of opportunities, hectic schedule, and the list goes on.

- **Fear of change**. It is quite natural to experience fear in the face of change, and usually the bigger the change, the greater the fear that must be dealt with. Personal development involves taking actions that make us feel uncomfortable, anxious, or inadequate. These types of emotions inspire fear of change. Imagine speaking publicly if you are an innate introvert, or a career move if you are someone that has a strong need for security.

- **Settling for mediocrity.** It's easy to perform beneath your abilities, capabilities, and talents. Many have compromised their true desires and aspirations to the point where they habitually settle for good results, when they could obtain excellent results.

Part 3
Guiding and leading crucial mentoring conversations

> *"A single conversation across the table with a wise a man is worth a month's study of books."* – Chinese proverb

Possibly the greatest challenge for mentors is to find time for crucial mentoring conversations. Every senior executive and manager that I consult with could easily fill each day twice over. For every possible entry into their diary, they are asking, "Does this align with my most critical priorities? Can someone else handle this? Can it wait a few weeks?" They invest their time in relationships only where there is tangible value for them and their business.

Value for time – even more than value for money – has become immensely important. If you want to successfully build strong relationships in mentoring you have to understand how to consistently add **value for time**. Mentoring needs to find time amongst an avalanche of internal meetings, emails and operational challenges and pressures.

Value for time could include both giving value and getting value from a mentoring conversation. A mentor is giving value when he is energising an important initiative, sharing some insight or experience, asking the right questions, and challenging his mentee to action.

On the other hand, the mentee is getting value when he gains valuable new information, being pushed to rethink a problem, getting perspectives broadened, or making a new personal connection.

For both the mentor and mentee, the concept of value and time are critical. (**You will note there is a statement in each conversation, "This conversation adds value…",** that describes what is in it for both parties. There will be no second chance unless there is value for time that can be extracted from the various crucial mentoring conversations. With this as a prerequisite, it is now useful to study the various crucial mentoring conversations covered in the book.

These are in no particular order and mentors and their mentees can decide what is most important or even appropriate from a timing point of view. A good starting point, however, will be a conversation on 'Purpose'.

Each of the conversation descriptions will cover the following:

- The focus of the conversation.
- The question that the conversation should clarify.
- The value that the conversation could offer.
- Some useful questions that the mentee might want to contemplate.
- A story from the mentor relevant to the conversation.
- Possible conversation outcomes/post conversation assignments.

Asking questions forms a significant part of each crucial conversation. Peter Drucker, renowned author and management consultant, observed that, "In the past managers were hired to tell people what to do. The leader of the past was a person who knew how to tell. The leader of the future will know how to ask the right questions".

Please note that the questions and even the outcomes from each crucial mentoring conversation only serve as a prototype of questions/outcomes that can be explored with your mentee.

Adapt the suggested questions to suit your mentee's situation. Keep in mind his age, level in the organisation, maturity and readiness, then consider the possible scope of questions that could be asked in each conversation.

Part 3: Guiding, leading crucial mentoring conversations

Conversation on purpose and vision

"Musicians must make music, artists must paint, poets must write if they are to ultimately be at peace with themselves. What human beings can be, they must be."
—Abraham Maslow

It is a privilege to live. Every day we are presented with a kaleidoscope of opportunities, choices and challenges, yet most of us have no clue what we want to do with our lives. This statement is not exclusive to those who have just finished school or started working. Even after we have earned decent salaries it might still ring true for most individuals. It's a struggle almost every adult goes through. "What do I want to do with my life?" "What am I passionate about?"

I changed career aspirations more often than my holiday plans. And even after I had established People's Dynamic Development, it wasn't until I was 32 and my two sons had been born, that I clearly defined what I wanted for my life. Part of the problem is the concept of 'life purpose' itself, whether you view this spiritually, personally or professionally. Here's the truth. We were born to live for some undetermined period of time. During that time we do things. Some of these things are important. Some of them are unimportant. The important things give our lives meaning and happiness. The unimportant ones basically just waste our time.

So when people say, "What should I do with my life?" or "What is my life purpose?", what they're actually asking is: "What can I do with my time that is important?" and "How can I be more meaningful?" This typically happens later in life, when we develop the need to give back, to be of service to the next generation, or to contribute to sustainability.

Thinking about death can produce a passion for life. We are ready to live our lives when we know what we want written on our tombstones.

That's a powerful thought! It forces us to review and assess our purpose as well as our goals, plans, and activities to get at the core reason of why we exist. Mentees become purposeful when they can express their purpose in the moment rather than working towards achieving it in the future. You have a sense of purpose when your life has a direction and meaning that you have chosen. Remember that purpose differs from vision, which is about what you want to create and achieve; you choose a vision but discover your purpose.

Here is a good example: My wife studied Finance. She has a strong financial background and worked in corporate finance for close to 15 years. She excelled and established herself as a valued partner. Eight years ago she founded a non-profit organisation that focusses on children's ministry in our community. She has discovered her purpose. Individuals who pursue their purpose:

- display focus;
- have the energy to pursue their dreams;
- display mastery in what they do;
- exhibit discipline in how they manage their time and priorities;

- show determination and resoluteness in dealing with day-to-day challenges; and
- demonstrate persistence and endurance.

Uncovering purpose and values

Purpose expresses who you are, who you are becoming, and what contribution you can make. Our lives become meaningful, at home and at work, when we align with our purpose.

Mentors can facilitate the discovery of their mentee's purpose by looking at the course of their lives, noting the themes and patterns that characterised their timeline, and noticing the qualities of those times when they felt most valued and alive.

Consider the Tombstone Test, i.e. what would you like your epitaph to be? Steve Jobs successfully lured John Sculley, then CEO of PepsiCo, to Apple. Sculley's sense of purpose was evoked when asked, "Do you want to spend the rest of your life selling sugared water or do you want a chance to change the world?" (Sculley, 1988).

One possible approach to a conversation on the topic of 'purpose' is to work with value priorities. Values sit at the gateway between our inner and outer worlds, and personal values are a central part of who we are and who we want to be. They describe what is fundamentally important and consequently meaningful to us, and so are directly related to our sense of purpose and to our needs. Values allow us to make the best choice in any situation. Some of life's decisions are really about determining what you value most. (*see the list of 100 most common values.)

Linking individual and corporate purpose

Organisations can also be described as having purpose, often referred to as the mission. Just as individual purpose can be accessed through personal values, so organisational mission can be accessed through corporate values. The fact is that values provide the link between the individual's purpose and the organisation's mission. The psychological contract, as we know it, between employers and employees, involves an exchange of time for pay. Our younger generations are demanding more from their employment than just financial rewards, however; they are pursuing the opportunity to develop and fulfil themselves. Organisations that are able to quench this aspiration for more gratifying work will be able to attract and retain the best employees. The challenge for organisations is to provide their employees with the opportunity for more personally meaningful work, whilst simultaneously enabling the organisation to meet its goals.

The role of the mentor is to assess this alignment and help the mentee to deepen their understanding of organisational reality, develop their sense of self-awareness, and encourage them to live their purpose and pursue their goals, dreams and aspirations.

A conversation on purpose should be seen as a discovery and learning process, not a problem to be solved. It takes a lot of time and thoughtful reflection to look deeply inside ourselves and answer the hard questions: who we really are, what our values and priorities are, and the trade-offs we are willing to make. Mentors might have to exhibit patience in having more than one conversation on this topic as the relationship and the mentee mature.

The focus of this conversation is to appreciate the purposefulness of your mentee and to acquire insight into their goals, dreams, ambitions and values.

It answers the basic question: What is important to him? Where is my mentee going or planning to go? Where does he see himself?

The conversation provides value as it allows the mentor to have a greater understanding of the life choices of the mentee and what motivates her. When you understand how your mentee acts, feels, and responds in situations, it can guide your interactions with them. For the mentee it provides an opportunity to gain clarity on purpose, vision and values.

Some questions to explore around this conversation – decide what would be most appropriate for your particular relationship:

- Share your most significant life decisions, i.e. family, partner, studies, job, career.
- What have the five most important events in your life been?
- Tell me about an accomplishment of which you are particularly proud.
- What makes you unique, e.g. values, interests, competencies and skills?
- What do you bring to a relationship that you know others appreciate or that others find meaningful about you?
- What drives you, gets you up in the morning, keeps you going?
- What fills your tank emotionally, physical and spiritually?
- What are your most important personal and professional goals right now?
- What are the short term goals that you have set for yourself? What assistance would you need to achieve these goals?
- How will you define your purpose?
- What would you want your family, friends and community to say about you upon your death? What about your team members, business partners, people in the organisation, customers you've served, or colleagues you've worked with? In the end, did you contribute to or take from society?

Possible mentoring story

Use your own life story or your personal and professional journey. Share the powerful shaping experiences in your life and possibly share why you do what you do.

Conversation outcome/assignment:

- Write a personal purpose statement.
- Ask your mentee to draw up a personal or life timeline.
- Identify their list of top ten values.

Remember the discipline to write it down is the first step to making it happen.

Creating a personal or life timeline

This exercise provides an opportunity for your mentee to reflect on their whole life, their time in a particular organisation, or even a job role. It also allows them to tell the story of their highs and lows, as well as their most important choices/decisions on a single path. It will further help your mentee to recognise achievements and challenges. Timelines are particularly useful if a mentee feels stuck or is uncertainty about what their purpose is.

Step 1

Create a lifeline on a large piece of paper. This lifeline might only reflect your mentee's professional life or career, but could also include key moments from school, college, previous employment, marriage, even moments of personal loss, health or other achievements. Reflect on the most important moments – highs and lows.

Step 2

Make a list of the most positive and negative events. Order them chronologically and annotate them with + for positive and – for negative. The timeline provides a pictorial view that can be more useful than a list of activities. It might indicate patterns or a series of negative events that provide the context to your mentee's low self-esteem or sheer determination to succeed.

A timeline provides an opportunity to grasp the magnitude of events and the impact and reasons for decisions. There are many ways to depict such a timeline. Allow your mentee to choose how graphic they want it to be and the extent of detail to include in the timeline. The means for completion is not as important as taking the time to reflect on this personal journey, and consider all the forces that got your mentee to where he is.

Part 3: Guiding, leading crucial mentoring conversations

Niël Steinmann's timeline:

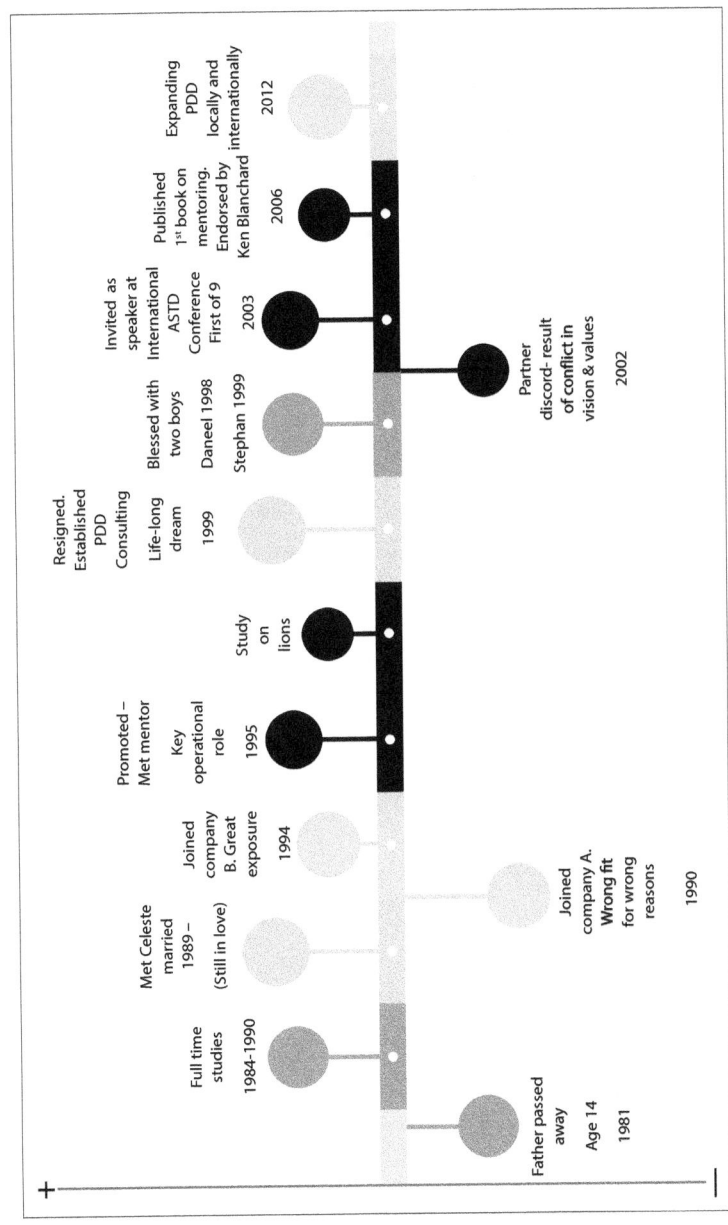

Your mentee could further share what he has learned from each event and how they dealt with both the positive and negative events..

- It could be interesting to view which of the events were a result of your mentee's discipline and choices, and which might be a result of poor relationships or wrong decisions at the time.
- What patterns are becoming obvious from the timeline?
- Discuss any outstanding events that might not have been listed.

Reflecting on values

A good way to identify the values that are most important to your mentee is to look back on his life – to identify when he felt really good and really confident that he was making good choices.

Reflect back on the timeline exercise and ask your mentee to identify times when he was happiest, proud and most fulfilled. Why is each experience important and memorable? Use the following list of common personal values to get started. Ask your mentee to identify and list the top ten values. Your mentee should then prioritise these values based on which is most important.

Discuss the outcomes and note these values that influence your mentee's decisions and life choices. See if there is a value alignment with that of the organisation's values. Talk it over.

List of the 100 most common values*

Accountability	Equality	Patriotism
Accuracy	Excellence	Peaceful
Achievement	Expertise	Perfection
Ambition	Fairness	Popularity
Assertiveness	Faith	Positivity
Balance	Family	Professionalism
Belonging	Fitness	Quality-orientation
Calmness	Freedom	Reliability
Challenge	Fun	Reputation
Cheerfulness	Generosity	Respect
Clear-mindedness	Goodness	Restraint
Commitment	Growth	Results-oriented
Community	Happiness	Security
Compassion	Hard work	Self-actualisation
Competitiveness	Health	Self-control
Consistency	Helping society	Selflessness
Continuous improvement	Honesty	Self-reliance
	Humility	Sensitivity
Cooperation	Independence	Serenity
Courtesy	Inner harmony	Service
Creativity	Inquisitiveness	Simplicity
Curiosity	Intelligence	Spirituality
Decisiveness	Joy	Stability
Dependability	Justice	Support
Determination	Kindness	Teamwork
Diligence	Leadership	Timeliness
Discipline	Legacy	Tolerance
Discretion	Love	Trustworthiness
Diversity	Loyalty	Truth-seeking
Effectiveness	Mastery	Understanding
Elegance	Obedience	Uniqueness
Empathy	Openness	Unity
Enjoyment	Order	Wealth
Enthusiasm*		Wisdom

*Some values missing from the list? Add your own.

Conversation on career momentum/mobility

"When one door closes another opens, but all too often there is a long hallway in between." —Rick Jarow (The Ultimate Anti-Career Guide: The Inner Path to Finding Your Work in the World)

Understanding the challenge of employability

The old paradigm has at last expired – you don't stay in a single career until you retire. The notion of lifetime employment has been replaced with lifetime **employability**. Let us first understand the difference between marketability and employability. This understanding is key for mentees before a mentor embarks on a conversation about career.

The Oxford Dictionary defines **marketability** as "the relative ease at which a commodity can be sold or marketed" or "an individual's attractiveness to potential employers". We can directly influence our marketability, for example we can obtain a degree in a relevant field. Some individuals are masters at the art of selling themselves in an interview. Surely it is important to be marketable? It enhances the probability of an application and provides an invite to the interview.

Employability, on the other hand, is a set of achievements; an individual's track record and personal attributes that make him more likely to obtain employment and to be successful in a chosen career which benefits themselves, the workforce, the community and the economy.

Often marketable people are successful over the short term, landing different jobs in quick succession. But here is the challenge: your reputation for excellence, track record, and value-add ultimately determine how successful you will be in your career. It is only when you are really employable that you are truly marketable – how you perform on the dancefloor might open future doors and more attractive invitations.

Tim Stevens, in his book, *Fairness is overrated*, spent a whole chapter on 'A Résumé is worthless', writing that, "almost all résumés contain two categories of information: education and jobs held. Yet when I am hiring, those are the things I care the least about. I much rather want to find out and check with references: leadership, track record, passion, attitude and character".

You can't rely on your employers to maintain your employment – you alone are responsible for your career progression and development. In *The Empty Raincoat*, Charles Handy skilfully phrased it as follows: "We are in fact all mercenaries now on sale to the highest bidder and only employable for as long as we have knowledge and skills that institutions can benefit from".

Career development is no longer only about gaining the skills and knowledge you need to move up within one company. You need to remain satisfied and fulfilled by the work you are doing, but it is also about achieving flexibility and continuously evaluating and developing your skills in order to remain employable and fulfilled over the long term, regardless of who you are working for and what industry you are working in.

To achieve this level of flexibility, you need to have a very strong sense of who you are and what you want from your work. Not everyone is motivated by the same thing, and our ambitions vary greatly. Some people thrive on having the freedom to be creative and innovative, whereas others prefer structure, stability and continuity. Being challenged and constantly stimulated may be important to one mentee, while creating a work/life balance and managing family realties is paramount to another.

For your mentee to effectively manage his career, they need to know more than what they enjoy doing – they need to understand WHY they like doing it. Your mentee will also need to figure out what the underlying characteristics of the work are that make it enjoyable, interesting and stimulating.

One of the most common questions that your mentee will seek guidance from you as a mentor on is: "How do I manage my career?" This is a fundamental aspect of an individual's professional life.

Why do people get promoted?

Marcus Buckenham raises a valid question in his book, *First break all the rules*, which will most certainly also feature in any crucial mentoring conversation on 'Fitness'. "When it comes to development, career growth, or praise, why do we so often resort to moving people up the ladder?" The fact is, most organisations keep promoting people because of a dangerous combination of assumptions.

1. The best performer will also be the best manager.
2. Future opportunities equals promotion, and if we don't promote people they will leave.

Individuals, on the other hand, often have the view that, "If I want to move onwards and upwards in my career, I **need** to climb the ladder".

The fact is, man has a desire for recognition and glory; a yearning for prestige. For some, prestige also equates to power over others. It is a fundamental human motivation, a craving for prestige and respect. In today's knowledge economy (and tight labour market) we should place a greater emphasis and reward on specialised expertise, knowledge and performance. Chances are good that the brilliant software developer, craftsman, designer or salesman knows more about their particular field or customer than their manager does. Promotion should not be seen as the only vehicle that will provide recognition or the means to a lifestyle.

Any conversation on career could lead to a myriad of much deeper conversations:

- Managing a career.
- How to get career direction.
- Developing a career strategy.
- Identifying career opportunities.
- Discovering career anchors.

This assessment of your mentee will provide you with further insight into his future goals and objectives. Encourage your mentee to think about how to enrich his role, move laterally, work off-shore, or take on a secondment to learn new skills. The ability to recombine skills, competencies and experience increases options to move between functions, divisions or even industries. We all need portable skills that will allow us to move from one industry to another.

Mentees could strategically map out developmental assignments and challenges, considering 'zig-zag' career paths rather than vertical ones. Technical and functional expertise will not be enough to move into managerial levels – strong **leadership** skills and business principles also matter. Promotion offers the opportunity to see the organisation more as a connected system, where one department's outputs become another's inputs.

Assess what your mentee has that fits with key business needs or is distinctive. Encourage them to initiate proposals for assignments, new learning or transfers. If need be, 'pitch' a proposal for an opportunity that would create new business advantages.

A massive concern is when your mentee has a series of roles and responsibilities that essentially repeat the same experience. This not only restricts the further development of a broader range of skills, but also impacts on their employability in the long term.

With the right planning your mentee can pursue ambitions, make their goals known, and design their career path.

The focus of this conversation is: To gain clarity on your mentee's career aspirations and motivation around mobility.

It answers the basic question: The conversation is not about how to get promoted, but rather "How employable is your mentee?" What is required to be successful in a particular career and how can he move his career forward?

The conversation provides value as it allows the mentor to gain an understanding of the career history, anchors and achievements of his mentee. It either validates or rescinds all career decisions the mentee has made. It further strengthens the mentee's professional identity and boosts their career development opportunities.

The sky's the limit when it comes to discussing a mentee's career aspirations. Depending on what is appropriate for your unique mentoring relationship, here are some questions to explore around this conversation:

- Does your current contribution promote your purpose, vision and values?
- How does your current job facilitate the development of core skills towards your vision and goals? What other exposure would you need?
- What are you currently enjoying/not enjoying about your work life?
- What value do you think you are adding?
- What do you miss in your current role?
- What are your career anchors? (*See list)
- What are your short and long term career goals? What support is needed?

- What plan do you have in place for your future growth and development and what is your level of commitment regarding your future development?
- What resources have you employed to facilitate your career plan?
- Do you believe you are visible enough in what you are doing, i.e. is your contribution seen and appreciated?
- What could you do to become more employable?
- What sacrifices would you be willing to make to pursue your purpose and goals?
- What can the company do to enhance your success or remove obstacles to your progress/career?

Possible mentoring story

Share how you got to where you are. Impart a lesson you have learned along your career path or mistakes that you feel you've made in your career that you feel would be helpful for your mentee to consider.

Conversation outcome/assignment:

- Ask your mentee to identify the key variables that will impact on his career.
- Does your organisation have a resource on career development? The mentee should work together with HR and complete any action items listed.
- Identify three career opportunities and prerequisites for success/progress, e.g. formal studies, specific exposure, organisational realities.
- Ask your mentee to complete 'career anchors' and work though the thinking of Edgar Schein (see below).
- After completing some of the above assignments, ask your mentee to write his résumé two years from now.

Discovering career anchors

The concept of **career anchors** was introduced by Edgar Schein. He suggested that "all of us have a particular orientation towards work and that we approach our work with a certain set of priorities and values". He called these "career anchors", which include the talents, motives, values and attitudes that give stability and direction to a person's career; it is the 'motivator' or 'driver' of that person.

Often, people select a career for all the wrong reasons, and find that their responses to the workplace are incompatible with their true values. For example, a challenging job that requires a 60 hour work week is incompatible with someone who has a high regard for work/life balance.

Completing an exercise on career anchors will allow you to understand your mentee's preferences, and will assist the mentoring relationship to plan a specific career in a way that is most satisfying to your mentee.

Table 3: Career anchors

Career anchor category (from Schein)	Traits
Technical/functional competence	Individuals like being effective and useful at something and will work to become a subject matter expert. They enjoy being stretched and will use their skills to meet the challenge.
Managerial competence	Some people want to be managers. They enjoy problem-solving and are comfortable dealing with other people. They thrive on taking up responsibility. To be successful, they need emotional intelligence.

Career anchor category (from Schein)	Traits
Autonomy/independence	These people have a basic need to work by their own rules and to get things done on their own. They dislike standards and prefer to work alone.
Security/stability	These people seek stability and continuity as a key factor of their lives. They avoid risk and would be comfortable staying in their job.
Entrepreneurial creativity	These people like to invent things, be creative and most of all to run their own businesses. They differ from those who seek autonomy in that they will share the workload. They find ownership very attractive and it is important to "do their thing".
Service/dedication to a cause	Service-orientated people are driven more by how they can help other people than by using their talents. They may work in public service or in areas where they can contribute to the well-being of others.
Pure challenge	People driven by challenge seek constant stimulation and difficult problems that they can tackle. Such people will change jobs when the current one gets boring, and they will explore other career opportunities.

Career anchor category (from Schein)	Traits
Lifestyle	These individuals highlights the importance of their world and style of living. They are more likely to integrate both work and personal life. They may even take long periods of time off work in which to indulge in passions such as travelling.

Conversation on performance

"It is no use saying 'I am doing my best'. You have to succeed in doing what is necessary." – Winston Churchill

Performance management is a practice for appraising whether an employee is 'performing' satisfactorily on the job. For organisations and HR, the process is moral and justifiable; the result from this measure is supposed to be used to assist the employee to become a better performer in his current position. Nevertheless, it epitomises one of the absurdities of corporate life. Managers and staff alike view performance management as time consuming, excessively subjective, demotivating, and ultimately unhelpful. In these cases, it does little to improve the performance of employees. It may even undermine their performance as they struggle with ratings, worry about compensation, and try to make sense of what they perceive to be an unfair system.

Mentoring is also a process for development, which raises the question, "Should mentoring be tied to an organisation's performance management system?" The answer in my view is "no", but also "yes". Let me explain. In mentoring, there is normally no reporting relationship between the mentor and the mentee, i.e. a manager would usually not mentor a direct report. (There are exceptions and I have witnessed a number of line-manager relationships that evolved into successful mentoring relationships). Mentoring is not intended to replace the relationship between an employee and his manager. Mentors in my view should not conduct or provide input to performance reviews.

Even though mentoring is not responsible for performance management, I would strongly recommend that mentors take their mentee's performance seriously. We all know the drill. Managers say some positive things about what the employee is good at, then some unpleasant things about what he's not good at, and then end with some more positive strokes to the employee's ego. The result: a mixed message that frequently leaves even your best employees feeling disappointed and confused.

The other reality is that success could make your mentee the target of nasty criticism. The sad fact is that we all have to navigate our way around opponents in our career: external critics, competitors, unpleasant and subjective bosses, or colleagues who undermine. Seasoned mentors understand that their mentee's performance can be scrutinised, and therefore their confidence should be enhanced by reflecting on and exposing them to both positive and more constructive messages and views of others.

Mentors explore opportunities to bring performance conversations to the table and ensure that there is a greater understanding of the 'mechanics' of performance management, but also identify specifics that could form part of the mentee's development plan for current and future roles.

Work performance

The focus of this conversation is: To have a greater understanding of the current level of the performance and contribution of the mentee. The focus is also on facilitating areas of both positive and helpful feedback.

It answers the basic question: How is my mentee doing/performing?

The conversation provides value as it allows the mentor to gain greater clarity of areas for improvement and on what to focus the attention. For the mentee it is a performance enhancer – it validates areas for amendment and also serves as a confidence builder by identifying where the mentee is excelling. Everyone wants to know how he is doing at his job.

Some questions to explore around this conversation – decide what would be most appropriate for your particular relationship:

- What were your successes last year? Share some detail.
- What were your disappointments last year? Would you like to share more?
- What lessons have you learned from your successes and disappointments?
- What value do you think you are currently adding? Do you believe you could add more?
- What were the obstacles to your performance? Self, team, leader, resources?
- What do you think people are saying about your performance, conduct and brand?
- How can we make sense of specific feedback that you have received (sometimes a mentee mulls over something that was said, that needs clarity or amplification).

Possible mentoring story

Share how feedback has shaped your personal development journey. Reflect on the best feedback you have ever received. Share how it made you feel and what you changed after that. Possibly share a story of negative feedback, the impact it had, and the end result.

Conversation outcome/assignment:

- Identify possible opportunities where your mentee's interaction with others could provide valuable feedback. It could be their attendance at meetings, presentations, or client interactions.

- Select three key stakeholders/role players in the organisation that would and could provide honest, constructive feedback on your mentee's performance, conduct or brand. Arrange for meetings or ask the mentee to set up these meetings. These individuals might be previous or current line managers, project managers, a key customer, or someone more senior in the organisation, e.g. a line manager's boss.

- Integrate feedback and identify: "What sense can we make from all the feedback?" Then identify strength areas, development needs and possible actions.

- Consider how you can facilitate more regular, accurate and authentic performance conversations between your mentee and other role players.

Rethinking performance – challenge the performance management paradigm

What usually comes to mind when we think of performance management is the formal HR system, which consists of steps, forms and procedures for conducting appraisals. A negative take on performance management is that managers place a substantial emphasis on financial rewards at the end-of-year performance assessment. This process holds their staff accountable for past behaviour at the expense of improving current performance and grooming talent for the future, both of which are critical for an organisation's long-term survival. However, research has shown that the greatest contributor to high performance does not lie in the application of the formal aspects of the performance management system, but rather in the quality of relationships and trust between employees and managers. This means we need to embrace the idea that performance management should not be just a once- or twice-yearly event driven by the formal system, but rather more regular critical reflections on behaviour for which everyone is responsible. This provides an opportunity for mentors to facilitate more frequent conversations on performance, which might also include informal check-ins between the mentee and his manager about their performance.

Feedback should closely follow the natural cycle of work. Ideally, conversations between mentors and mentees should occur when projects finish, milestones are reached, challenges pop up, and so forth – allowing people to solve problems in current performance while also developing skills for the future. A performance conversation should be more holistic, not just about past performance, but also about attaining business goals and contributing to the organisation's success.

Frequent, informal check-ins will lead to more meaningful discussions, deeper insights, and greater mentee satisfaction.

Useful pointers on feedback:

- **'Feedback'.** The word says it all. It is a gift so think about how you give it. Often feedback tells us far more about the person giving the feedback than the person receiving it.

- **Change your language.** Stop using the words "negative feedback". Negative means "undesirable", "harmful", "damaging", "depressing" and "destructive". No wonder people respond to negative feedback the way they do. How about "helpful" feedback? This means "accommodating", "supportive", "caring" and "beneficial". Next time you are about to give feedback, ask yourself, "Do I feel "negative" or am I ready to be "helpful"?

- **Do it early.** Don't wait to provide feedback. Too often mentors ignore what bugs them, but then the mentee does the same thing again (and again). The more you delay saying something about it, the more annoyed you'll become and the less patient and effective you will be when you finally need to be "helpful" in your feedback.

- **The power of the spoken word.** Words have power with the ability to help, to heal, to hinder, to hurt, to harm, to humiliate and to break confidence. Considering the powerful force of the words we utter, we must discipline ourselves to speak in a way that conveys respect, gentleness and humility. When you say something like "You're unprofessional", it's a recipe for disaster. A character attack provides no information, it warrants a response, and it doesn't offer any actionable ideas for change.

- **Speak to the person's interests.** Mentees will consider changing if you speak to their interests. Show them how changing their behaviour will help them and tell them why you are giving them this feedback, for example you're doing it because you have an interest in them achieving, or because you are concerned about possible perceptions, or because you care about their well-being and success.

- **Practice authentic compliments.** You will notice I have not used the word "paying" compliments. A true compliment is given freely with no expectation of anything in return. Make sure that you're doing so because someone or something truly deserves recognition, and not just because you want to fill the silence or seem polite. It might be qualities that you admire, a change in behaviour or just a stunning shirt. Keep it short and don't overdo it.

- **Think "feedforward".** Marshal Goldsmith believes that feedback only deals with the past. He suggests the practice "feedforward", which is about providing individuals with suggestions for the future to help them achieve a positive change in behaviour. The idea is not to critique or to bring up the past but to focus on future behaviour, i.e. "Next time you present I would like to see if you could...".

Part 3: Guiding, leading crucial mentoring conversations

Conversation on fitness

"The meeting of preparation with opportunity generates the offspring that we call luck." – Anthony Robbins

What got you here won't get you there is a thought-provoking book by Marshal Goldsmith. He proclaims that people get promoted because of their technical competence, i.e. the good engineer becomes the engineering manager, the good accountant becomes the financial manager, and the good teacher eventually becomes the school principal. The notion that he shares is about the danger of overpromotion or "The Peter Principle", which describe how most employees are promoted to a level of incompetence. What made you successful in your previous job most definitely does not make you successful at the next level. Those promoted spend their time differently and potentially spending less and less time doing the things they are truly good at or passionate about.

So why do organisations keep on promoting good employees who become poor managers or incompetent leaders? The answers are often: "We want to see people grow", "We want to offer them better opportunities and a career", "We want to reward them for their extraordinary efforts and performance" and "We want to retain them". People can grow, learn, be challenged and even develop their careers without being promoted. And so the question remains: "Why do we keep promoting people just because they were excellent in what they were doing?" And why don't we make a greater effort to assess the potential, readiness or the fit based on the individual's strengths for the next level?

My prediction is that the "Peter Principle" will 50 years from now be as deeply ingrained in organisations' thinking as today, unless we make a more intentional effort to include strengths-based career development and conversations on 'fitness' as part of a 'test' to assess the readiness of staff.

Mentors could play a proactive role preparing their mentees for the next level or any new role/career opportunity by having this conversation. Capabilities that signal that your mentee can move to the next level might include business acumen, strategic thinking, an ability to build a cohesive team, knowing when to change or innovate, tolerance for and the management of risk, getting things done across silos, influencing and being a positive influence, clear and confident communication, and organisation specific leadership competencies. This should be an ongoing process and not something that only happens when the role/position they want emerges.

The focus of this conversation is: To a have a broader understanding of the workplace skills required at the next level or for a specific opportunity that the mentee has in mind. The previous crucial conversation on performance is a check in the mirror on how your mentee is doing; it is reflective. This conversation is a forward check to see how ready your mentee is; it is a forward-looking conversation.

It answers the basic questions: How ready (adaptable and committed) is my mentee for the challenges and opportunities that are lying ahead?

Are the reasons why they are interested in the next level a financial consideration? Is it about prestige and recognition, or is it a naturally strengths-based career development and progression?

The conversation provides value as it is a proactive tool to explore the readiness of the mentee. It provides an opportunity to assess capabilities and competencies. It is a deep dive into, "What will be required?" Identifying the mastery of key academic, technical and workplace knowledge, skills and dispositions that vary from one job to another is crucial. It also provides a greater understanding of how the organisation calibrates talent and where the mentee features within the system.

Some questions to explore around this conversation – decide what would be most appropriate for your particular relationship:

- If you were promoted tomorrow into the (….) role /level/job, what would you find most difficult to deal with?
- Based on the first question, what are the technical competencies (i.e. job specific) and possible development activities?
- Based on the first question, what are the professional competencies (i.e. leadership) and possible development activities?
- What learning activities could develop these competencies?
- What are the challenges that you face in achieving the above?
- What have you done during the past 12 months that is promotion-worthy? How did you meaningfully contribute to business results?
- How would you be able to help the organisation better if you were in a more senior position?

Possible mentoring story

Share a true story of how someone's confidence or aspirations were affected by a too early or too fast career progression.

Conversation outcome/assignment:

- Identify what targeted development activities are required to accelerate your mentee's readiness for the next level role.

- Have a conversation on where your mentee is on the company's talent grid. Identify specific development needs and opportunities.

- In the absence of a talent grid, assess the competencies and job specific requirements for a specific or next level job and assess your mentee's readiness on each key competence and prerequisite.

- Ask your mentee to list the extraordinary achievements he has accomplished in the past year and additional responsibilities taken. These should be things that set him apart from other candidates for the position. Focus on what advantages these had for the company, not on how much of a personal sacrifice they were.

Prerequisites for 'fitness' conversations

Does your organisation take the development of their bench seriously? Organisations that are most successful at securing strong bench strength are those that clearly value talent from the moment they step into the door. Once the right talent is on board, the onus is on senior leaders and mentors to begin cultivating the talent bench. Securing a deep and talented bench requires a relentless focus on grooming high potentials, an initiative that should be sponsored directly from the top. It is a tough job to have this conversation with a mentee when the organisation is not taking talent seriously.

Does your organisation calibrate talent/fitness?

The most conventional technique for succession planning and employee development conversations is the 9-box talent grid which plots employee performance against potential. This technique is a strategic tool for identifying and developing talent, not only at an executive level, but for everyone in the organisation — regardless of his position, length of service or location.

Part 3: Guiding, leading crucial mentoring conversations

Working collaboratively, managers arrange every employee into one of nine types across a vertical and horizontal axis, based on three levels of performance and three of potential. Some organisations take it a step further to define potential that is reflected in their future needs, i.e. learning agility, leadership, and contribution to business growth.

Line managers then use these descriptions to plot an individual in a specific quadrant to determine a variety of outcomes. The 9-box grid should be used as a tool for talent calibration, rather than as a tool for labelling. Determining readiness can be influenced by many factors outside an employee's capability, including location, position/level, career stage, and diversity quotas (gender, ethnicity, age).

Together with managers, mentors should determine a list of possible development actions, including feedback, assignments, and possible next level exposure that will be of greatest benefit to the individual and organisation. Mentors need to monitor and review employee plans and progress, follow up with a fitness conversation, and meet regularly where necessary (e.g. monthly) to fine-tune development strategies.

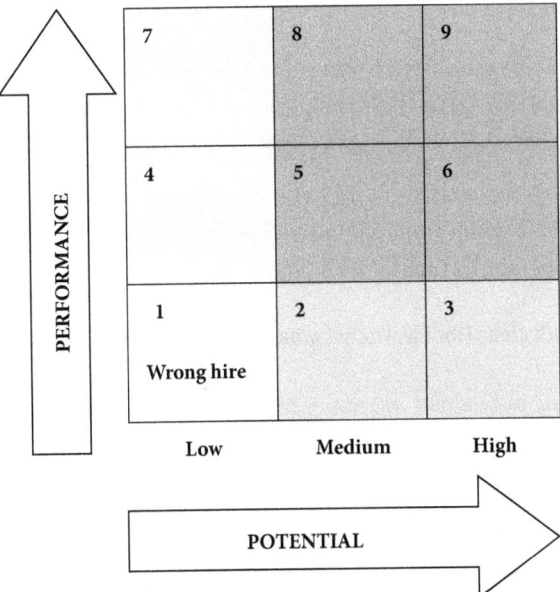

Figure 2: Talent grid

The low potential group

1. These are underperformers who show limited potential. Managers need to agree on actions and outcomes or manage their exit from the business.

4. This group consists of average performers. They show little ambition but meet the basic requirements to do their job. They will possibly stay in the same job forever. Managers could challenge them to improve in their current role.

7. This group includes value-add performers who are at the end of their stretch. They love their job and could be stretched with development initiatives that take their functional competence to an even deeper level. For them, the future holds the same type of job and similar team roles.

The low performance group

1. As discussed previously, managers should seriously consider terminating this group as their tenure is not sustainable for any business.

2. These are poor performers who show medium potential. They could potentially be in the wrong role and may need to be assessed and coached. Again, managers might have to manage their exit.

3. This group consists of underperformers with lots of potential. They could benefit from intentional mentoring and conversations on career momentum.

Talent bench group (the ideal target group to mentor for future development)

1. These individuals are core employees and consistent performers who meet all targets. Often not enough is done on the training and development of these individuals.

2. These individuals meet all targets and demonstrate great potential. They are possible candidates for future promotion and should benefit from the crucial mentoring conversation on fitness. There is

still room to improve performance, however they are valuable assets for the future.

7. These individuals normally exceed targets and will respond to stretched goals and greater challenges. Mentors need to facilitate development opportunities. They would benefit from crucial conversations on feedback and fitness. These individuals are possibly experts in their functional areas who may or may not want to move into leadership. Development should focus on specific gaps, i.e. what is needed to broaden or to move to the next level of responsibility.

8. These are the organisation's top talent and star performers, who are often referred to as 'key retains'. This group includes strong candidates for promotion. These individuals will benefit from accelerated development initiatives and should intentionally be included in strategic and leadership initiatives.

Conversation on strengths

"Human Resources are like natural resources: they're often buried beneath the surface and you have to make an effort to find them."
– Sir Ken Robenson

Gallup's research shows that globally, only 20% of the employees working in the large organisations that were surveyed indicated that they use their strengths every day. It is fascinating that the longer employees stay with an organisation and the higher they climb the typical career ladder, the less likely they are to strongly agree that they are playing to their strengths at work. The challenge for organisations and you as a mentor is to focus inward to the great wealth of unrealised capacity that resides in every single employee and mentee.

According to Marcus Buckenham in his book, *Now discover your strengths*, most organisations are built on two flawed assumptions about people:

1. Each person can learn to be competent in almost everything.
2. Each person's greatest room for growth is in his areas of greatest weakness.

The fact is that most organisations take their employees' strengths for granted and focus on developing or at least minimising their weaknesses. To break out of this, mentors should change and challenge their assumptions about their mentees. Here are two principles to consider:

1. Your mentee's talents and strengths are enduring and unique.
2. Your mentee's greatest growth could be in the areas of his strengths.

Gallup defines a 'strength' as the ability to consistently provide near-perfect performance in a specific activity. They also define talents as "naturally recurring patterns of thought, feeling, or behaviour that can be productively applied". This means that a knowledge base, talents, and skills – along with the time spent practicing and developing skills – combine to create strengths. Talking with your mentee about his strengths is one of the best ways to grow a greater understanding and appreciation of strengths.

The focus of this conversation is: To assist mentors to recognise the talents of their mentees and how they fit in with their different roles. Mentors must further explore the convergence of these talents and personal passions.

It answers the basic questions: What is my mentee's competitive advantage? What is he capable of being and doing with his life?

The conversation provides value as it allows an opportunity to accelerate development, boost confidence, and multiply the innovation and creativity of the mentee. Mentees will be able to benefit from this fundamental truth: "Confidence comes from competence".

Focussing on your mentee's strengths is an **ACCELERATOR**.

Your mentee will grow faster and develop more in the areas of his strengths than in his development areas.

Developing strengths is a **MULTIPLIER**.

We are all more creative and innovative in the areas of our strengths than in our development areas.

Developing strengths is a **BOOSTER**.

We are more inclined to bounce back from failures in the areas of our strengths than in our development areas.

Developing strengths is a **CONFIDENCE BUILDER**.

It is a simple fact. Confidence comes from competence. If you are confident without being competent then you are arrogant. The flipside of the coin is that our development areas or 'weaknesses' erode our self-assurance and confidence.

Some questions to explore around this conversation – decide what would be most appropriate for your particular relationship:

- What has been a lifelong passion area or interest? What do you love to read (professionally)?
- What do you do best?
- What is an area where you are considered to be an expert? The area where you are the go-to person on your team?
- Which areas of your work do you love doing the most or look forward to doing?
- What type of work do you find the most rewarding in your day?
- Have you noticed that certain types of work make you tired/drain you, even though you might be good at them? What type of work would naturally fall in this category?

- What is the best way to keep you challenged?
- Are you in the right territory? Can you play to your strengths in the territory?
- Which skills and competencies can you leverage better to make an even greater contribution to the business?

Possible mentoring story

You could share a metaphor from nature or sport on the value of 'playing to your strengths'; no animal in nature can survive in a territory that does not complement its strengths. As a matter of fact, they strategically pick a territory that suits their strengths. A territory that complements strengths enhances the prospect for survival, as well as the procreation and sustainability of that species.

Conversation outcome/assignment:

- Ask the mentee to complete a strength finder assessment and discuss the results.
- Examine your mentee's personal strengths and passions, then assess how well they are being leveraged and possible next steps.
- Explore possible relationships that could provide insight concerning your mentee's strengths. Gain feedback or comments about whether his current function is realistic and the best way to use his talents.

So what about your mentee's weaknesses?

This conversation on strengths does not mean we ignore our mentees' development areas. No matter how distinct or powerful your mentee's strengths appear, his weaknesses could be intimidating to develop. Weaknesses drain confidence and amplify the awareness of what we are not capable of doing, thus mentors should focus on strengths and find ways to manage weaknesses.

First let's define a weakness. The simplest definition in my view is anything (thinking or behaviour) that can hamper or get in the way of excellent performance. You will note that we all have countless areas where we are not proficient or skilled. These areas may even affect our self-regard and sense of worth, however they are not necessarily weaknesses. I am, for instance, not good at working with my hands. This lack of talent or skill is simply not worth bothering about. It is not a weakness because it has no bearing or impact on my ability to consult or to run a consulting business. If I struggle to convince others or lack self-belief… well, that is something to take more seriously. The cornerstone to greater performance lies in confidence, and mentors cannot ignore those areas that validate your mentee's or even their line manager's concerns. For example, if your mentee alienates those around him, some feedback or even training might be useful as it could potentially harm his future ambitions or success.

Conversation on relationships

"You are only as happy as the relationships you are in." – Anonymous

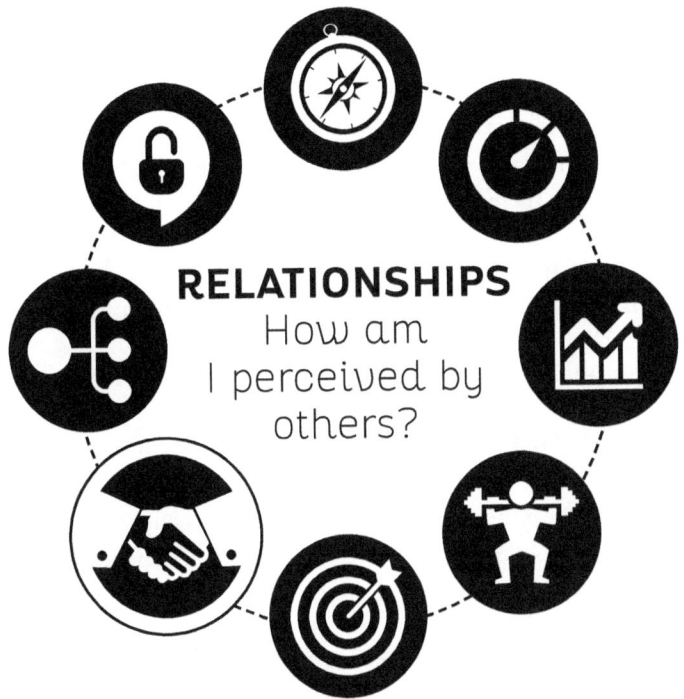

The above quote confirms that life is all about relationships; some of our greatest moments of joy, and even misery, happen socially, professionally and even publicly. It is indeed a challenge for most people to build strong, healthy, effective relationships. Daniel Goleman, the original researcher in the field of Emotional Intelligence, defined relationship management as the ability to be aware of the emotions of those people you interact with, and along with your own emotions build strong working relationships. It includes aspects such as conflict management, team work, collaboration and how effectively you communicate.

That's a tall order, but fortunately those skills can be taught and learned. Should your mentee master these skills, they will have more success in their relationships – at work with direct reports, co-workers, teammates, and customers, and at home with their spouse, children, family and friends.

As you progress in your career you collect 'labels' – "He's a great manager, but lacks new ideas" or "She's good at strategy, but can't sell the idea". When your mentee's name is mentioned during a talent review session, what goes through other's minds? Whether it is fair or unfair, perception is reality. If there are deep-seated perceptions about your mentee they may have been formed over years, so it will require a visible and consistent effort to change them.

The focus of this conversation is: To understand the importance of relationships and look at ways to build beneficial relationships.

It answers the basic question: How is my mentee perceived by others?

The conversation provides value as it allows the mentee to identify his relationship needs and consider ways to build profitable relationships. It is also to develop the necessary people skills to manage the challenges that diversity poses. This means culture, religion, gender, generations, even diversity in personality and thinking styles.

Some questions to explore around this conversation – decide what would be most appropriate for your particular relationship:

- What do you stand for? Who do you want to reach?
- What do you want to be known for?
- What is your reputation/brand?
- What type of people do you find difficult to get along or work with?
- What characteristics do you believe make up good relationships, e.g. trustworthy, honest, respectful, listener, embrace diversity, caring, open communication?
- Ask your mentee to select from the list which quality he views as the most important and to rank them with regards to his abilities.

- What is your view on leadership? What makes someone a good leader?
- What is your style of leadership? How effective do you think it is?

Possible mentoring story

- Practical examples about your own relationship point of view as a mentor. Your toughest relationships that you had to deal with and the outcomes.
- Various relationships and how to manage them.

Conversation outcome/assignment

- With your mentee, identify at least three individuals who he finds challenging; individuals who may be difficult to work with, report to, or manage/lead. Discuss the way to overcome this.
- Have your mentee complete an Emotional Intelligence assessment. Ensure that a qualified practitioner gives the feedback and contract your attendance or ensure that the results are made available to you.
- Complete a Johari Window. Ask your mentee to Google the model. It is a self-explanatory model and a great tool with which to create understanding and self-awareness, with a focus on personal development, improving communications and nurturing interpersonal relationships.

The Johari window

The Johari window was created by psychologists Joseph Luft and Harrington Ingham. The four Johari Window perspectives are called 'areas' or 'quadrants'. Each of these quadrants contain and represent the information – feelings, motivation, etc. – known about the person, in terms of whether the information is known or unknown by the person and by others in the group.

- Assess how your mentee deals with conflict. Identify specific situations or relationships that will benefit from more effective conflict handling strategies.

- Identify three relationship management skills with your mentee that he would need to work on. Ask for action plans.

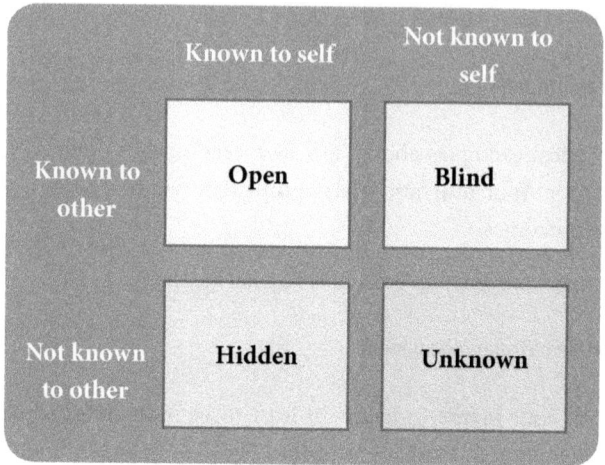

Figure 3: The JOHARI-window

- The open window relates to things that both you and your mentee know about him.
- The hidden window relates to things your mentee knows about himself but has not disclosed to others.
- The blind window relates to how others perceive your mentee that he is not aware of.
- The unknown window relates to things in your mentee's unconscious that you are also not aware of.

These windows allow you, as a mentor, to explore relational issues. You could explore how large these panes are for different relationships. They further allow you to be aware of what you are told in the open by your mentee and what your mentee is not telling you. It is also important to identify where your mentee is unaware of his behaviours, feelings and emotions, but how others experience or perceive these behaviour or actions.

Discuss your mentee's relationship with various role players, peers, supervisors and subordinates. Explore the relationships that work and those that do not. Recognise any insights that will enhance current and future relationships.

Taking the sting out of conflict

One of the most important skills your mentee needs to learn and develop is how to deal successfully with conflict. Successful individuals seem to have an inherent understanding of what causes conflicts and how to resolve them quickly. For others, however, it's much harder as they are caught up in this whirlpool of perceptions and emotions.

There are healthy and unhealthy ways to respond to conflict. Reflect with your mentee and assess which column reflects the most accurate behaviour when he is confronted with a conflict situation. You might want to mark this page because I predict that you will need it somewhere in your mentoring relationship. Do this assessment when your mentee is confronted with an actual conflict situation.

Table 4: Conflict assessment

Unhealthy responses to conflict	Healthy responses to conflict
Takes things personally and feels hurt by what was said.	Demonstrates the ability to take the emotions out of the conflict situation.
Loses objectivity and in the process the conflict escalates.	Has an inherent understanding of what caused the conflict and remains objective.
Blames the other party. Has a strong desire to prove the other wrong and point out their mistake.	Reflects on own contribution to the conflict and recognises how own behaviour and mistakes led to the conflict situation.
Reacts in the moment; says the unsayable.	Responds by how the other person makes them feel. Shares the emotions experienced.

Unhealthy responses to conflict	Healthy responses to conflict
Unable to recognise and respond to the things that matter to the other person.	Shows capacity to recognise and respond to the things that matter most to the other person.
Explosive, angry, hurtful, and resentful reactions. Use of strong language.	Calm, non-defensive, and respectful reactions. Uses 'soft' answers.
The withdrawal of love and attention, resulting in rejection, isolation and shaming.	A readiness to forgive and forget, and to move past the conflict without holding resentments or anger.
An inability to compromise or see the other person's side.	The ability to seek compromise and avoid an "eye for an eye" mentality.
The fear and avoidance of conflict; the expectation of bad outcomes.	A belief that facing conflict is the best thing for both sides.
No solutions, only justice.	Looking for solutions and willingness to solve.

Reflect with your mentee on the 10 golden rules for conflict management.

Don't expect to be loved and appreciated by everyone

The Bible says "In this world you will have trouble". This definitely does not only refer to passing exams, finding employment, suffering from illness or the loss of loved ones. It most certainly refers to the fact that we share the planet with seven billion other people, i.e. we do not live our lives in isolation and where there are people, there are different personality types, opinions, and viewpoints. The other reality is that no matter how hard you try, there will be those who do not like you, who might treat you unfairly or with disrespect. With that realisation, we have a responsibility to manage those dislikes and disagreements with compassion and wisdom to bring about the best resolutions possible for our mentees.

Never respond in a moment of anger

Walk away if necessary. While this is not easy to do because we are biologically primed to fight or flee, sometimes not reacting is incredibly effective. Decide not to respond in the moment. This requires strength, patience, wisdom and a detachment from your ego (it is the ego that "takes it personally" and gets hooked during conflict). Calm down and cool off. Then write that e-mail but don't send it. Read it again the following morning and you will be surprised to see how much of the content you should phrase differently. It takes years to build a reputation and five minutes to lose it. Think about how you respond!

Acknowledge own emotions and seek discernment about your planned reaction

We need to acknowledge and understand what emotions are evoked by each conflict situation. Are you angry because it's not fair? Are you disappointed because the individual has let you down? Are you hurt because of what was said? Are you bitter because you are holding on to hurt? Keeping this broader perspective during conflict helps your mentee to focus on self-awareness, self-management and social awareness, resisting the impulse to react purely based on the emotion of the moment.

Resolve conflict hastily

Knowing that most people don't like conflict makes it even more imperative that we learn to deal with disagreements as quickly as possible. People generally have a strong fear and dislike for confrontation. They confront the issue only when they feel someone has completely overstepped or they grow frustrated enough. If we settle small, simple disputes immediately, they never grow into something that festers and becomes a bigger problem. But when we don't deal with a situation quickly, we dwell on what we should say and how we were offended, and it snowballs from there. Strong disputes develop, leading to hurt feelings that could potentially destroy relationships.

Care to look through other's lenses

There are many factors, including upbringing, cultural background and past experiences, that shape our lenses on how we see the world. One person's background may be that he did not grow up understanding what peaceful conflict resolution looks like, while another person may believe from experience that people cannot be trusted. When we care to look through another person's lens, we slowly begin to understand their perspective and why they act, think and behave the way they do. It's a little like putting on another person's spectacles. It may be difficult to see at first, but if you keep them on and allow your eyes to adjust, you slowly begin to see the world the way they see it — however imperfectly — through their lens. When we consider another perspective, it's easier to engage in gracious, passionate debate without disrespect or insults.

Think about the words you choose and how you say them

Most conflict situations happen not because of what is said, but because of how it is said. Conflict does not have to be drama-filled; shouting and swearing only contribute to an escalation of the conflict, and to try to run someone's name or reputation into the ground only makes the matter worse. Before you toss those verbal grenades ask yourself: **"Is it true?", "Is it necessary?", "Is it kind?"** I have been a part of many sharp disagreements that resulted in no hard feelings. Handling conflict provides an opportunity to listen, allow rigorous debate from all sides, and respectfully consider how we respond and what we say. Then our arguments can be peacefully resolved and your relationship will deepen.

Look for positives from the conflict

Ask "What have I learned from this?", "What did I learn about myself in this situation?", "What do I understand better about the other person or group?", "What can I appreciate about the other person/party?" There is always something to take away from a conflict situation. Remember, you can achieve more with an honest enemy than a false friend.

Stand up for what you stand for and stand by it

If you know why you do what you do and say what you say, you will be honest in trying to live by those values and standards. You can be confident in any conflict if you stand up for what you believe in and know is right. Be predictable. When someone tries to solicit a response or raise a contentious topic they need to know what reaction they will get from you. You don't need to apologise for it or fight for your views and opinions. You could even agree to disagree. The moment you are dishonest or make it up as you go along, you will have big problems dealing with the conflicts that come your way.

Don't stick your nose in it

Being the mediator is not always easy; often it invites trouble and frustration. Unless you want to lose your nose, you shouldn't stick it into someone else's conflict. That does not mean you can never fulfil the role as peacemaker, but avoid offering advice without someone asking for it. Make sure you listen to both sides. Conflict is often the result of failure to see the other's perspective. When you moderate with that in mind, try to see all sides through the individual lenses represented.

Say it!

There are times when we need to say "I am sorry", and mean it. We cannot always be right. There are times when we mess up, say the wrong things, do something that we thought was right at the time, or just make the wrong judgement. Admit that you are human and susceptible to mistakes, then ask for forgiveness. Such an apology reveals a heart of remorse.

Ask your mentee to commit to three strategies that speak to them personally. Remember we are all a work in progress, and by committing to possible strategies we are improving our maturity and character to deal with conflict and to improve relationships.

Conversation on networks

"Behind every great leader, at the base of every great tale of success, you will find an indispensable circle of trusted advisors, mentors and colleagues." – Keith Ferrazzi

People are more successful in life and at work when they are connected to, and in contact with, a trusted collection of like-minded individuals. Mentors understand that the real path to success, personally and professionally, is through creating an inner circle of "profitable relationships" that are "valuable, productive and gainful".

Earlier in the book I suggested that mentees should be encouraged to build multiple relationships from which they can benefit. Meaningful relationships should be established with a few key trusted advisors who will offer the encouragement, feedback, and generous support that every one of us needs to reach our full potential. The reality is that no one person can have all the answers. The complexities of our world and the pace of change mean that no one is qualified enough for us to entrust our career expectations and development journey to a single or lifelong mentor.

Mentees should look for mentors, advisors and sponsors who can have a stake in their success or failure. A mentor will help you find your path, an advisor will help you make the right choices on the journey, and a sponsor will open some doors on the journey. Having an influential sponsor is an enabler that could accelerate opportunities, but it requires consistent performance to get a mentee on the sponsor's radar.

From first time job seekers to CEOs, they all need 'profitable' relationships. Without investing in developing and growing these mutually beneficial and trusted relationships, mentees are unlikely to survive.

The focus of this conversation is: To explore the diverse relationships that your mentee should manage and leverage.

It answers the basic question: With whom should my mentee network and build alliances?

Who are the contacts? The acquaintances for specific things.

Who are the connectors? People who know the right people.

With whom to build alliances? People to have on your side.

With whom to partner? People who bring specific skills, competencies or resources to the table.

The conversation provides value as it creates an opportunity to strategically understand that "your network is your net worth". It allows the mentoring relationship to explore and identify areas both personally and professionally, where other role players could provide assistance, knowledge, insights, and wisdom to the mentee. Seasoned mentors realise they can't do it alone; they expose their mentees to their extended network. These networks may facilitate new opportunities, quicker responses, greater understanding, opening of doors and the removal of obstacles.

Some questions to explore around this conversation – decide what would be most appropriate for your particular relationship:

- Explore specific areas where networking or alliances will significantly contribute to your mentee.
- Who is currently in your inner circle? Who should you have there?
- Who are current and future sponsors?
- How do you nurture and keep your relationships and networks alive?
- What do you have to offer to your network? (It is about giving before you can receive.)
- Who are the 'yes men' who make a lot of promises but do not add value?
- With whom should you build bridges proactively, even before you need them?
- Who are the other mentors and coaches that your mentee potentially needs to connect with?
- How do you employ specific social media as a tool to establish a greater, more credible network?

Possible mentoring story

A story about the most connected person you know and how he connects or leverages various relationships, both personally and professionally

Conversation outcome/assignment

- Take a specific challenge that your mentee should implement. Ask them to prepare a scenario of who to include in the "meeting before the meeting".
- Create a network mapping chart and look at ways to build and manage various relationships.
- This should also include clients and customers. Good relationships with clients and customers can also lead to extra business or revenue, career advancement, and a more rewarding career.

Embrace the "meeting before the meeting" principle

This is a timeless yet essential principle for anyone looking to have a successful meeting about a contentious issue. The "meeting before the meeting" could even be considered a strategic opportunity to gather information, to network, and to build rapport, trust and alliances. That way, by the time the actual meeting happens, your mentee has a well thought out set of justifications for his point of view.

Any time your mentee wants to start something new, implement an idea, ask for budget approval or make a change, he should consider who are:

1. the individuals who have a different point of view;
2. the role players who are the most vocal on the relevant topic; and
3. the individuals who have the most political influence — even if their own area won't necessarily be affected.

Then ask them what they think, for their ideas, what questions they might pose, what concerns they might want to address, or what additional information they would need. Not only will your mentee rally each of them to his cause, but in the process, he will gain valuable information about what and how to communicate in a more formal setting.

Create a network mapping chart

Encourage your mentee to show interest in other people and ask questions. Urge them to find out how they can be of help to others. How to follow up and stay in touch. Almost everything they achieve will be the result of the people they meet and the relationships they form along the way.

During a mentoring relationship, there could be a number of discussions about the extended network of your mentee. A relationship mapping chart can be useful for both you and your mentee.

The technique involves using mind-mapping principles to create a visual image of the people in your mentee's mentoring relationship network.

Crucial mentoring conversations

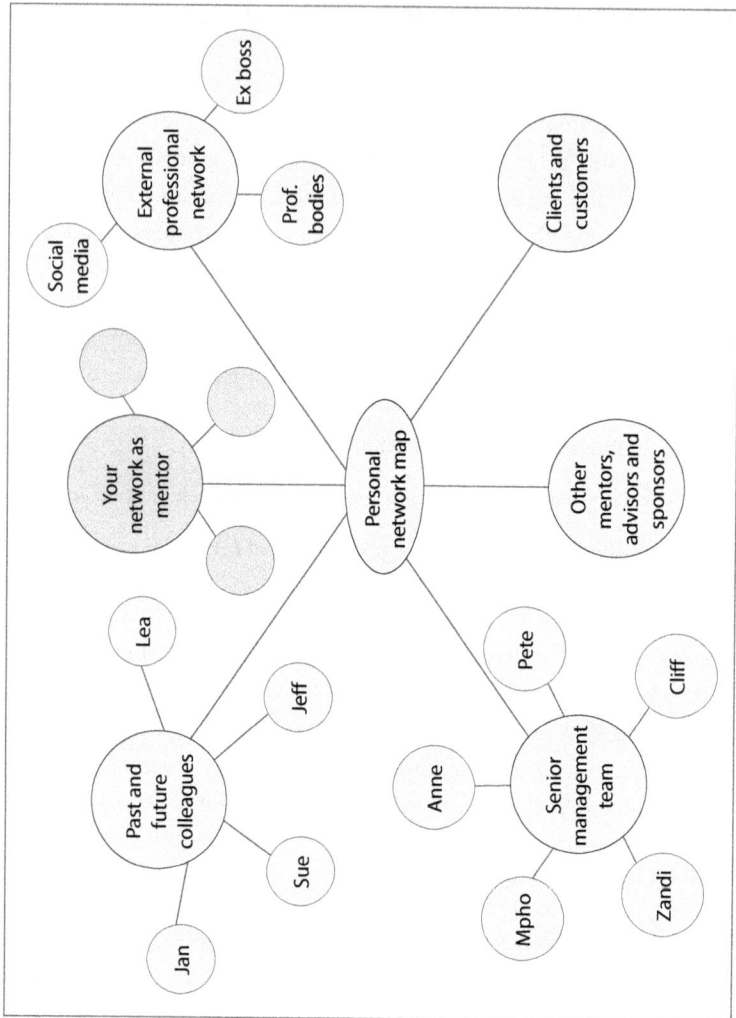

Figure 4: Example of a network map

You can imagine that such a chart for your mentee would be more complex, but this gives you an idea of how your mentee could construct such a map. There are a number of purposes and benefits of such a map:

- It provides a visual picture of the various relationships that form part of your mentee's network. The use of various colours could provide further insight into which relationships are well established and which would require greater energy and connection.

- It provides a greater understanding of the position, impact and inter-relationships amongst various role players.
- It allows an evaluation of the extent of strategic relationships that might provide access to resources, further connections or opportunities.
- It could highlight specific actions that the mentee needs to take to work on these networks, e.g. making sure that he is invited to key meetings where he could contribute. He could also stay back after a meeting to continue conversations.

You could ask your mentee to add notes in all sort of ways:

- Who your mentee views as the most important contact for his short-term success.
- The depth and quality of the relationship network. Do they cut across managerial levels and divisions?
- Identify the network relationship your mentee would like to prioritise.
- It is most definitely not an exercise to see who your mentee can get something from. It will also be useful to see how your mentee could contribute to the various relationships in his map.
- Networking requires hard work but also an understanding that your mentee needs to learn to build bridges before he needs them.

The above is a real eye opener, and mentees will confirm that they underestimated both the number and complexity of the relationships in their network.

The dangers of social networking

Social networking is the practice of expanding the number of one's business and/or **social** contacts by making connections through individuals, often through **social** media sites such as Facebook, Twitter, LinkedIn and Google+. This changing world has brought new opportunities but also pitfalls, and potentially tons of negative publicity if used carelessly.

Employers increasingly base their hiring decisions on what they see on social media rather than on the content of a résumé. There are countless stories of people losing their jobs, health insurance claims and even their relationships because of something on social media that seemed totally innocent at the time. It is obscene the level of personal privacy we have given up in the 21st century without understanding the true ramifications.

We think we are in a safe and private place when we are connected, yet we are actually in a very crowded room surrounded by hundreds, if not thousands, of people, anyone of whom may, or may not, be listening in on your conversations.

Even those who are not on your circle lists (i.e. friend lists on Facebook, followers on Twitter, etc.) can still listen in to your conversations via wall posts and general tweets, responses to other tweets, etc. Imagine the following: if you are in a restaurant with your partner having a conversation over dinner, it is reasonable to assume that if you are not careful, those at the tables around you, even though not specifically involved in your conversation, can still hear what you are saying. The same with social media, except it is not so much your volume as it is the 'where' and 'what' you are posting that matters more.

So let's review then:

- 'Trolling' is the term for writing malicious comments to upset other people. Remember, any thought, view or opinion that is not carefully considered could have dire consequences – both personally and professionally.

- 'Going viral' can be a complete nightmare. Never do, post or say anything on the internet that you would not want repeated over and over again and which you would not do in public.

- Everything that goes on the internet stays on the internet, probably forever as far as you are concerned.

Part 3: Guiding, leading crucial mentoring conversations

Conversation on classified issues

"Feelings are much like waves, we can't stop them from coming but we can choose which one to surf." –Jonatan Martensson

Mentors understand that people do not leave their emotions at home or at the door when they come to work. Even though many organisational cultures place a high value on intelligence free of emotion, our emotions are often more powerful than our intellect. Scary thought, isn't it?

Mentors understand that when people are anxious, alienated, frustrated, or uncertain, their work suffers. They can't think as clearly, take in information as fully, or remain objective and respond as effectively when they're upset. For this reason, the mentor needs to cultivate moments that could create understanding or an opportunity to voice rather than ignore people's feelings.

Mentors understand that positive feelings motivate, build trust, create a sense of engagement, and increase confidence. There are great benefits to be had when feelings are understood and managed appropriately.

Mentors will openly admit that their success lies in the quality and the depth of their relationships. To understand the mentee, to be aware of the complexities and challenges that he faces, and to know their vulnerabilities, are priceless factors that contribute to profitable mentoring relationships.

Mentees expect their mentors to keep information confidential. If you stand by your convictions and your mentee knows they can trust you, they will have more respect for you and it will open the door to deeper, more intimate, discussions. When trust is broken, it is difficult to build it back up and mentees will stop coming to you with problems. Avoid gossip and confront any issues yourself, directly with your mentee.

When mentors share their own vulnerabilities or provide open and honest feedback it often sets the tone for a mentee to open up and disclose confidential matters. Get your mentee to take off the mask when he speaks to you.

The focus of this conversation is: To create a platform and a safe place to talk about specific realities, opportunities and challenges.

It answers the basic question: Are there any matters that my mentee would like to discuss off the record?

The conversation provides value as it allows the mentoring relationship to grow. It creates opportunities for greater mutual understanding and the appreciation of a magnitude of factors that may impact the life of your mentee. Remember, knowing someone at work is only one part of who they are!

Some questions to explore around this conversation – decide what would be most appropriate for your particular relationship:

- Are there other factors that potentially impact on your current performance or future decisions?

- What is holding you back?
- If you could change one thing, what would it be?
- What is that one decision that you would like to reverse?
- What do you find stressful about your work?
- What makes you lie awake at night?
- If there is one thing that you could share that would make others understand you better, what would it be?

Possible mentoring story

Sharing a personal life story is often a powerful way to facilitate a conversation that allows for openness, greater transparency or truth. Here is my story: My father's passing (I was 14 at the time), the circumstances around it (he died in my arms of a heart attack), and how we as a family had to come to terms with it, shares some valuable life lessons and more so, something about who I am today. Remember that our personal journey, successes, failures, rejections, personal losses, health, financial difficulties, and relationship challenges make us uniquely able to provide value to someone who is challenged by similar moments. We can really only offer condolences if we have experienced loss ourselves; we can only advise about raising children if we have had our own. There is a better understanding of why people respond to the news of cancer if you have had a personal experience or someone close to you has. So this story could be something confidential, something you have not shared with a lot of people, but in the moment, your story might open the world to your mentee.

Conversation outcome/assignment

Be prepared, your mentee could disclose career opportunities and job offers. They could open up and share previously withheld information, suppressed feelings and possibly fears. Organisational politics and perceptions, and even family and personal circumstances, could be discussed. All these topics provide opportunities to strengthen the relationship.

Hold your mentee accountable for any possible actions or next steps as a result of these confidential discussions.

Remember that your mentoring relationship should have boundaries. Do not try to solve issues that you are not qualified to intervene in; you are not a marriage councillor, a family therapist, a clinical psychologist or a behavioural specialist who is able to professionally diagnose or recommend treatment.

Part 4
Pouring yourself into someone

Mentoring high performers

Mentoring high flyers, i.e. those identified for fast tracking, or any mentee that has been identified for succession planning, requires mentoring with great care. These relationships could be complex due to the mentee's elevated self-belief and high expectations that the organisation set. The mentee's high expectations could make it the relationship tricky to facilitate. Your credibility and confidence as a mentor will be vital to build a profitable, trusting and respectful relationship.

So how do you pour yourself as a mentor into such a challenging relationship? As a mentor, you should understand the DNA and behavioural traits of any high achiever.

Ambitious mentees have a strong desire for success and are highly motivated to achieve success. It is a privilege to mentor such individuals who are inspired to follow their dreams, but believe it or not, I have learned that too much ambition is also dangerous. When a mentee is too ambitious they lose all sight of practicality, could become indecisive, and sometimes won't commit to long-term jobs/projects.

How do you as a mentor deal with over-ambition?

- Your mentee must understand that pursuing his ambitions requires balance. Life and its responsibilities will always be there; it doesn't disappear.

- In order to follow his dreams your mentee must factor practicality into their ambitions, otherwise he will end up frustrated. The younger generations feel pressured to rush and pursue success quickly, but success does not always come in the next quarter, year, or two years.

- Assure your mentee that in order to do his absolute best and make something great, he needs to do everything at a measured pace with a lot of devotion. Encourage him to measure things out, devote time working on the intricate details, and patiently wait for things to be fully done.

High achievers tend to be competitive and self-assured. They are normally keen to learn new skills and will be on the lookout for new learning opportunities to improve themselves. They are confident in their own area of expertise and will demonstrate their skill and capacity with confidence in a wide range of business scenarios.

How do you as a mentor deal with an over confident mentee?

- Over confident mentees often exhibit a dark side that they are not necessarily aware of. They could act in a way that makes them appear arrogant, selfish and even aggressive. This tendency for star performers to only think of themselves makes them forget that they cannot make it on their own. Subtle feedback should encourage them not to alienate colleagues or potential sponsors.

- Highlight the dangers of relying too heavily on one particular skill or strength, or even one sponsor or mentor, as this could derail their aspirations.

- Discuss possible de-railers. The importance of a cultural fit, expectations within the organisation, as well as how your mentee is perceived, should be discussed. If you know that the management team views your mentee as arrogant and a big talker, it requires attention and a crucial mentoring conversation.

- High achievers are sometimes blind to their own development needs, which is why mentors should be courageous and willing to highlight the perceptions of others or the mentee's opinion of himself.

Vast expectations result in goal-driven behaviour. Being selected as part of a talent pool or succession group in itself creates expectations from a mentee's perspective. High achievers want to be stretched to achieve goals and need challenging assignments to have the feeling of constant growth. They are eager to compare themselves with other's advancement and constantly want to check their readiness for progression.

How do you as a mentor deal with high expectations?

- Ensure that there is a clear understanding of your role and value proposition.
- Mentors need to encourage their mentees to be grounded and to focus on the opportunities of the moment.
- Reflect on the fact that career development is not a race but an intentional effort to leverage strategic opportunities for one's own path. It should be a longer-term focus and development goals should be encouraged.
- Never shy away from tough conversations. It is important to help a high achiever to identify possible blind spots or self-limiting beliefs, as these areas often hamper growth opportunities.

A number of the mentoring skills and techniques have already been covered in the book, but there are a few points to re-emphasise.

- The success of any mentoring endeavour lies in the quality of the relationship. Mentors should cultivate trust and make an effort to establish a connection with their mentees. Mentors are expected to model the way around a number of competencies, for instance if the mentee needs advice on how to deal with issues during a board meeting, they would typically expect their mentor to have substantial board level experience.
- Contract specific outcomes and possible measures for success. Discuss the possible crucial mentoring conversations and discuss the process that will be most functional to adopt during the mentoring relationship.
- High flyers love to be challenged, so encourage them to explore, improve and develop, but make sure that you fully leverage your network to facilitate conversations and/or exposure to opportunities. Remember: You don't learn to swim by sitting next to a pool reading a book on swimming. The best way to learn is to experience it – to be in the water.

- The type of questions that you as a mentor phrase to your mentee require depth, consideration and insight. For example:
  - If you could swing the proverbial magic wand, what are the three most critical aspects that you would like to improve on within the next three months?
  - Imagine you are promoted and will be starting in your new role as from tomorrow. Which areas/aspects will you find the most difficult or challenging to manage or deal with?
  - List the activities/issues you have already handled which would be considered to be more within the realm of the position you aspire to be promoted to.
  - Next time we meet have some ideas ready to talk about that you think you could pursue to the betterment of the company if you were in a more senior role. Processes, technologies, leadership role etc.
- Assist them to see the actual outcomes from the different conversations and look at ways to incorporate the learning into their day-to-day lives.
- Provide regular feedback about actual progress. High performers need feedback to track their growth, as well as to evaluate if their hard work is paying off.
- Allow your mentee to take the lead to establish the agenda for any session. 'Watch with your ears' for clues that will indicate that your mentee is ready for the next topic or conversation that will add value.
- Mentoring high flyers can be incredibly rewarding, and mentors themselves will be stretched and challenged. Share your own experiences and acknowledge the value you get from the process. Not only does it show your commitment to the process, but also that the relationship is reciprocal.

Challenging comfort zones with the best intentions

Challenging your mentee is, in my view, part of a mentor's responsibility. It is a delicate skill and needs to be handled with lots of wisdom. To set a challenge could sound as if the mentor disapproves of the status quo, which could be perceived as negative. I encourage mentors to talk about 'challenge' as part of the mentor contracting to ensure that mentees are cautioned about this aspect of their mentor's mentoring approach. A challenge at the right time encourages mentees to step out of their comfort zones. The skill is not to intimidate but to say to the mentee, "I believe you can do more", "I would love to hear your opinion", "I believe you are ready for this, just do it ".

Mentees set self-imposed limits for themselves; they might doubt their own abilities, believe that they are not ready, or just simply overestimate the challenge. Mentors need to support and encourage. When mentees see that their mentors believe in them, they are more willing to step into the unknown.

When there are no challenges from the mentor then the mentee could become complacent. Mentors need to know their mentees well enough to identify the opportunities and when they are more than likely ready (in the right frame of mind) to be stretched. It could be a new assignment, meeting up with someone they have deliberately ignored, a presentation to clients, or taking responsibility for a specific outcome that should be achieved. Mentees often operate in high pressure environments that constantly change; their skillsets are challenged and there is a lot at stake with little margin for error.

Mentors need to be cautious not to fall into the trap of over-challenging their mentees, however, as this inevitably erodes confidence and a mentee's default setting, and insecurities may kick in to slow down the progress and good work that has been done. So how can you be more sophisticated?

Listen, don't judge, and resist the temptation to fix. Make sure that your mentee feels that he is supported and that they are not thrown into the deep end.

Remember there is a difference between "exposure" and "exposed". Which one of these two words would you feel most comfortable with in an unfamiliar situation?

"Exposure" is a well-planned effort to introduce someone to an action or situation, while "exposed" is the act of subjecting someone to an action or situation in an unprotected and revealing way. Mentors facilitate exposure without exposing their mentees, for example:

Scenario 1. A mentee is asked to attend a budget meeting because his manager has other commitments. He attends without any detail or being properly briefed on the figures or questions he could expect. That mentee would be **exposed**!

Scenario 2. The mentor has carefully planned the introduction of his mentee to a budget meeting. The mentee is coached and checked to be conversant and properly briefed on what to expect. The purpose of this planned **exposure** is twofold: to provide a learning opportunity for the mentee, and to ensure that key role players are introduced to the mentee and his potential value to the business. That is great exposure!

Questioning can also be employed as a powerful tool:

- Ask searching questions – "How would you justify this particular item in the budget?"
- Probe with clarifying questions – "Explain to me what that would look like if implemented?"
- Ask creative questions – "How would you go about tackling the issue if there were funds available?"
- Ask reflective questions – "You said that you felt exposed during that presentation. What exactly were you feeling and why?"

- Questions verifying maturity – "If you could do it again, what would you do differently?"

- Empowering questions – "If I gave you the go-ahead today, considering the options mentioned, what would be your next steps?"

Recognise when to "go off-line"

Here is a simple rule to consider. When you read it, you will probably think this is so obvious and so ridiculous to write about it, yet it is, in my view, one of the greatest blunders we make in modern times. We take our relationships or a potential misunderstanding with someone and CC, post or tweet about it. Once it is public, it has the potential to go viral and it is hard to stop something that you desperately want to withdraw. Here is the simple rule: We should never email, post a comment, or tweet about any relational conflict. What is the alternative? Talk to the individual in person so that you can see the eyes, the non-verbal cues, and break down the barriers introduced through technology.

Reading your e-mail I have no idea what you intend. This is especially true in the pithy thumb written smart phone world that we operate in. If at all possible, during times of misunderstandings, take the communication with your mentee off-line for a week and see how the relationship improves.

In Poverbs it says "a gentle answer turns away wrath, but a harsh word stirs up anger", especially if the interaction is from some device or platform. I have seen so many situations where an e-mail or message is misinterpreted, then spirals out of control and hurtful words are said in the moment of anger. Remember, no technology software or media platform can resolve a disagreement like face-to-face interaction; I call it "The value of smelling someone's breath".

The most common mistakes that mentors make

Low expectations for the mentee?

You can't mentor someone if you do not believe in them or see their potential. Goethe said "Treat a man as he is and you make him worse than he is. Treat a man as he has the potential to become and you make him better than he is". In Peter Senge's *Fifth Discipline*, he discusses the Pygmalion-effect and the power of self-fulfilling prophecies, and how often, whether they are positive or negative, they can really create a cycle of success or failure. The fact is, what we believe about our mentee's will influence our actions. Mentors need to have strong belief in their mentees and push them to do better. Believing that they can reach this expectation is only the first step, but I think a necessary one. This does not mean that all your mentees will become the CEO or own their own companies, but they can become better and more confident, pursuing their passions, strengths, and love for what they do.

Mentors acting as guides

It is not your job as mentor to fix, solve, control or be accountable. Mentors are tempted into the role of a 'guru' – someone who should have the answers to the mentee's questions – so they will listen, give answers, share anecdotes, etc. This is where the problem begins - the mentor is essentially acting like a 'guide'. When mentors act as guides, they put themselves in the position of having all the answers. As a result, the person they lead may grow – but passively. Avoid taking responsibility for your mentee's issues. Mentors do not have the best answer or solution on every topic. Period. Keep in mind that this process is about the mentee. When mentors share what feels like the right answer, they actually deprive their mentees of the opportunity to think for themselves. Don't rob them of that experience. Instead, nudge them by asking tough questions so they can figure it out on their own. The reward is twofold – you don't steal their revelation, and they hone a necessary life skill.

Underestimating the effort

A mentor sometimes say yes without a clear understanding of the time and effort that will be required or the specific needs of the mentee. Any strong relationship requires a solid foundation of mutual trust, understanding and respect. The most important thing you can do is to make yourself available and give your mentee some of your valuable time and your full attention.

Hiding your mistakes

Mentors are role models and facilitators, and in some cases those come into conflict. Trying to be a perfect role model can inhibit your ability to be a good facilitator; sharing experiences and failures in an honest and vulnerable manner can be more beneficial to your mentee than you may imagine. Openness, even about mistakes, ultimately makes you an authentic and better role model.

Not managing expectations

We live our lives trying to fulfil expectations, both our own and others'. Sometimes mentoring expectations can be overwhelming, but ignoring them won't make them go away. Mentees often have abstract expectations – too often they are not clearly defined nor expressed. In fact, they might initially be vague or even expectations created by the organisation. Just imagine the expectations that come with being elected to be part of an accelerated development or a management development programme.

Mentors must take the time right at the start to clarify expectations and responsibilities with their mentees in order to maximise the mentoring relationship. Spell it out and discuss and agree on how you could contribute, then "contract" the way forward. Is it to improve job performance, provide professional assistance, support career growth, or explore promotion opportunities?

Evaluating the impact of your crucial mentoring conversations

Formal/structured mentoring must have an end, as this allows the participants to assess the impact of both the mentor's and mentee's efforts, and evaluate how profitable the relationship has been.

As for the objectives set at the beginning of the relationship, mentors and mentees need to ask the following questions:

- What have we accomplished?
- Have we succeeded in what we initially set out to do? (Think about the initial objectives that were set at the start of the relationship.)
- What have we learned during this process or from our relationship?
- How can we apply the lessons and the knowledge we have gained?
- What are the core skills that the mentee has acquired?
- What have been the key take-aways for the mentor, both personally and professionally?
- How will the relationship describe the benefits of the crucial conversation process?
- Is there a need to continue informally?
- Are there any outstanding actionable items?

In conclusion

This book serves as a tool to make your mentoring role a personal priority and a value-add learning experience. I would like to leave you with a few thought that summarise the thinking around crucial mentoring conversations.

- Mentoring is, in my view, a powerful growth experience for both the mentor and mentee.

- The success of mentoring lies in the relationship – you cannot succeed as a mentor without 'connecting' with your mentee. The commitment of both mentor and mentee is a key element of a profitable mentoring relationship

- Successful crucial conversations hinge on a reflective process that begins with self-learning.

- Crucial mentoring conversations can only ensure sustainable change if the relationship stays focussed on shifting conversation to action. The true measure of a crucial mentoring conversation is the resulting action that it produces.

- Mentoring that is intentionally grounded in questions and principles of learning will become profitable for both the mentor and mentee.

- Please note that when you mentor someone, it is by no means a guarantee of promotion. Rather, it should mean increased breadth and depth of skills and experience to ensure that your mentee is more equipped for any possible career opportunity. Think of how the process has contributed to your mentee's employability.

In all these mentoring conversations, mentors attempt to create alignment and agreement by fostering open dialogue. Mentors should be intentional and consider the following:

- Ask yourself, "What is it that I would like to know and understand better from and about my mentee, and what would I like my mentee to appreciate and understand about this particular conversation?"

- Think about your personal view on a specific conversation and the lessons you have learned.
- Ask yourself, "Am I the right one to have this conversation with my mentee? Who in my network could contribute or provide a similar view to reinforce what I am saying or who could provide a completely different perspective to allow for out of the box thinking?"
- Contract with your mentee – how formal or informal should the conversations be, i.e. should my mentee journal their insights and capture their key teaching moments?
- How much preparation should there be for the conversations, i.e. should your mentee answer some of the conversation questions prior to the meetings?
- Lastly, remember that these crucial mentoring conversations should enhance accountability, improve performance, and ensure greater proactiveness and execution. These are all measurable elements that allow you and your mentee to assess progress, recognise small wins, and celebrate milestones and achievements.

Crucial mentoring conversations allow you as mentor to:

- spend time helping your mentee to discover the parts of their job that energise them and provide them with the most satisfaction. Explore with them their purpose, vision and values. Intimately understanding your mentee's hopes, dreams and goals, ultimately discovering your mentee's purpose;
- strengthen your mentee's professional identity and boost their career development opportunities. Explore with them their career aspirations. What do they hope to achieve? What are their aspirations? Are they realistic and achievable? Help them set career goals and understand their career anchors. What development will be necessary? Guide them in your experience on how to be more visible and what exposure will be most appropriate and relevant;
- provide quality feedback and honest evaluations on efforts and work completed. It nurtures an understanding of what the measures for

performance are and how others see your mentee's performance. You could also unpack how to assess performance management and encourage ways for your mentee to gain from positive and helpful feedback;

- promote opportunities to be more proactive. Mentees are encouraged to assess their fitness or readiness both physically and mentally for the next level or any new role/career opportunity that they may aspire too. It is a deep dive into what will be required in the future;

- potentially minimise weaknesses and amplify the talents and smarts of your mentee. Help them to discover their strengths, as focussing on strengths provides an opportunity to accelerate their development, boost their confidence and multiply their innovation and creativity. Mentees will be able to benefit from this fundamental truth: "Confidence comes from competence", and it allows the mentee to work/play in a territory that complements their strengths.

- Encourage a mentee to value their colleagues, note how they are perceived by those closest to them, and cultivate healthy relationships. Share their blind spots or any behaviour/conduct that could promote or hinder current or future relationships. Assist them to reflect on how they deal with conflict and to look at actions to improve those real life conflict vulnerabilities.

- Explore and identify areas both personally and professionally, where a network of other role players, mentors, advisors and sponsors could provide assistance, knowledge and new opportunities to the mentee. Mentors expose their mentees to their own extended network. These networks may also facilitate quicker responses, access to resources, removal of obstacles and opening of doors.

- Discuss classified matters. This will bring an appreciation for the magnitude of factors that may impact the life and performance of your mentee.

On reflection of these conversations, you might consider a number of issues or topics that were not covered, such as practical challenges or performance issues that you faced as mentor. These conversations do not provide a definitive list of topics or tools, but rather an opportunity to highlight or group those crucial mentoring conversations that could contribute to profitable mentoring relationships.

There are many other useful tools on the market that will allow your relationship to assess specific aspects of your mentee's profile, preferences and personality. Some of these are easily accessible using the internet, while some require specialists to allow for interpretation and a debrief.

- **Myers Briggs type indicator.**

  This is an extremely valid and reliable tool that identifies an individual's basic preference of four key styles and a description of their personality type.

- **Emotional intelligence assessments.**

  There are various on-line assessments available that will provide accurate feedback and recommendations on how your mentee can manage emotions and connect more skilfully with others, especially when he is under pressure.

- **Strength finder assessments.**

  Help your mentee discover what they do best.

- **Brain profiling tools.**

  This will lift the lid on your mentee's preferred way of thinking and in doing so help them to harness the power of whole-brain thinking.

- **Hogan personality inventory.**

  This describes how your mentee relates to others when he is at his best. It will also give you valuable insight into how he works, how he leads, and how successful he will be.

- **Belbin team type questionnaire.**

  Belbin empowers individuals to fulfil their potential at work and helps to bring together the right people to form high performing teams.

Crucial mentoring conversations

These assessments can provide your relationship with a wealth of information and will add to the quality of the various crucial mentoring conversations. All of these tools can assist to raise greater self-awareness. My wish is that you will find the time and a way to bring these crucial mentoring conversations to life. My experience is that they are potentially value-adding interactions for both a mentor and a mentee.

For me, mentoring is a way of life, a passion and a profession. For you, it might be a role that you as a manager are expected to fulfil, or possibly you recognise the importance of giving back or even leaving a legacy. Nevertheless, however you are involved in this role, my advice is the same – be committed, make time and do it intentionally. Mentoring is a joy and a massive privilege.

"You can retire from a job, but don't ever retire from making extremely meaningful contributions in life." – Steven Covey

References

Brown, B. 2013. *The Power of Vulnerability: Teachings of Authenticity, Connections and Courage.* Louisville, CO: Sounds True Publishers.

Clinton R., & Stanley, P. 1992. *Connecting: The Mentoring Relationships You Need to Succeed in Life.* Colorado Springs: NavPress.

Covey, S.M.R. 2008. *The Speed of trust: The one thing that changes everything.* New York, NY: Simon and Schuster..

Dent, F.E., & Brent, M. 2015. *The leader's guide to coaching and mentoring: How to use soft skills to get hard results.* London: Pearson.

Emilo, R. 2015. *Modern Mentoring.* Alexandria, VA: ATD Press.

Gallo, C. 2016. *The Storytellers Secret: How the World's Most Inspiring Leaders Turn Their Passion Into Performance.* New York: St. Martin's Press.

Hagel, J., Seely Brown, J., & Kulasooriya, D. 2014. *Shift Happens: How the World Is Changing, and What You Need to Do about It.* New York: Idea Bite Press.

Handy, C. 1995. *The Empty Raincoat. Making sense of the future.* London: Random House Business.

Johnson, H.E. 1997. *For Exceptional Performance.* Glendale, CA: Griffin Publishing Group.

Lombardo, M. 1996. *The Career Architect Development Planner.* Minneapolis: Lominger Limited.

Peter, L.J., & Hull, R. 2011. *The Peter Principle.* London: Harper Business.

Senge, P. 2006. *The Fifth Discipline: The Art and Practice of the Learning Organisation* (2nd ed.). New York: Random House Business.

Schein, E.H., & Van Maanen, J. 2013. *Career Anchors: The Changing Nature of Careers Self-Assessment.* San Francisco: Wiley.

Stevens, T. 2015. *Fairness is Overrated.* Nashville: Nelson Books.

Szczyglak, G. 2016. *How to be a brilliant mentor.* London: Pearson Publishers.

Taleo Research. 2011. *Profitable Talent Management.* San Francisco: Taleo.

Zachary, L.J. 2011. *The Mentor's Guide: Facilitating Effective Learning Relationships* (2nd ed.). San Francisco: Jossey Bass.

Index

A

abilities, 4, 33–35, 41, 46, 57, 59, 61, 78, 88, 90, 97, 100–102, 105, 126, 130
abundance mentality, 15
accelerator, 98
accountability, 44, 133
action plans, 103
actions
  anticipated, 59
  clear, 60
  planned, 59–60
  possible, 49, 86, 120
administrators of mentoring programmes, 14
advancement, 23–24, 123
advisors, 3, 110, 114, 134
  trusted, 59, 109–110
age, 30, 41, 65, 72, 93
  fit, 44
agenda, 4, 12, 36–37, 57, 125
  client's, 3
agreement, 42, 58, 132
  formal, 15
alignment, 20, 23, 69, 132
  institutional, 23
alliances, 17, 26, 32, 110–112
ambitions, 30, 69, 77, 79, 94, 100, 122
ambitious mentees, 122
anger, 105–106, 128
application, 3, 5, 12, 76, 87
  computer, 22
application value, 45
aspirations, 9, 40, 61, 69, 92, 123, 133
aspiring mentees, 38
assessments, 78, 104, 136
  end-of-year performance, 87
  on-line, 135

assets, 43, 66, 75, 83, 89, 95–96, 100, 109, 117
attendance, 86, 102
attraction
  mutual, 4, 12
  relational, 20
attractiveness, 52
  individual's, 75
authentic compliments, 88
authenticity, 49, 52–54
authentic mentoring relationships, 10
authentic mentors frame, 53
authentic relationships, 56

B

baby boomer, 6
balance, 122
  delicate, 4
  work/life, 7, 77, 81
behaviour, 23, 31–32, 37–41, 53, 58–59, 87–89, 97, 99, 104–105, 123
  changed, 42, 59
  past, 87
  unacceptable, 23
  unproductive, 56
behavioural traits, 122
behaviour match, 53
Belbin team type questionnaire, 135
beliefs, 10, 33, 39, 48, 105
  self-limiting, 124
  strong, 129
benefits, 5, 9, 16–18, 20, 22, 27, 30, 53, 56, 76, 95, 97, 110, 131, 134
blind spot awareness, 45
blind spots, 134
  possible, 124
blind window, 104
blocks, 55

Index

stumbling, 23, 41
board level experience, 124
board meeting, 124
booster, 98
boundaries, 50, 120
9-box grid, 93
brainstorming, 27
brand, 86
  personal, 32
bridges, 111, 115
budget, 22, 39, 57, 127
  request, 47
budget approval, 112
budget meeting, 127
building confidence, 21, 27, 38
business, 5–6, 9, 11, 13–14, 18, 23, 26, 30, 42, 54, 64, 82, 94–95, 99–100, 116
  extra, 112
  modern, 10
  strategic, 12
business acumen, 90
business and entrepreneurial skills, 8
business coaches work, 3
business excellence, 17
business executives, 19
business exposure, 17
business goals, 87
business growth, 93
business interests, 8
business knowledge, 39
business landscape, 24
business partners, 70
business performance, 3
  improved, 12
business presentation, 22
business principles, 78
business relationships, ordinary, 13
business scenarios, 123
business uncertainty, 22

C

candidates, 92
  possible, 95
  strong, 95
capabilities, 61, 90–91
capacity, 11, 18, 105, 123
  unrealised, 96
capacity building, 13
  mentee's, 19
career, 5, 8, 16, 26, 30, 43, 47, 49, 70–71, 75–81, 84, 90, 101, 112
  person's, 81
  single, 75
career advancement, 112
career anchor category, 81–83
career anchors, 78–81, 133
career aspirations, 17, 133
  changed, 66
  mentee's, 79
career challenges, 42
career decisions, 79
career development, 76, 80, 124
  strengths-based, 90–91
career direction, 78
career expectations, 5, 110
career goals, 30
  long term, 79
career growth, 77
career history, 79
career ladder, 11, 96
career level, 10
career mobility, 20
career momentum, 20, 43, 66, 75, 83, 89, 95–96, 100, 109, 117
career move, 61
career path, 7, 79–80
career plan, 80
career progression, 76
  fast, 92
career stage, 93
career strategy, 78

caring, 40, 88, 102
carte blanche, 30
celebrate milestones, 133
celebrate progress, 15
CEOs, 37, 68, 110, 129
challenging comfort zones, 126
change business focus, 22
character, 16, 39, 50, 76, 109
  favourite, 35
  fortifies, 40
character attack, 88
chart, 114
  network mapping, 112–113
  relationship mapping, 113
choices
  making good, 73
  right, 110
choices/decisions, important, 71
classified issues, 117
classified matters, 134
clear agreements, 58
client interactions, 86
clients, 2–3, 112, 114, 126
  important, 24
clients and customers, 112, 114
clients deepen, 2
clinical psychologist, 120
cloning efforts, 55
coaches, 3, 21, 26, 111
coaches partner, 2
coaching, 2–3, 26
  workplace, 3
coaching approach, 2
collaboration, 31, 101
collaborative learning environments, 26
collaborative mentoring approach, 19
collaborative relationships, 27
comfort zones, 126
commitments, 18, 27, 32, 34, 40, 42, 58, 60, 80, 125, 127, 132
  joint, 39

committing, 39, 109
communities, 10, 37, 67, 70, 76
company, 2, 7–8, 16, 24, 27, 30, 72, 76, 80, 92, 125, 129
compensation, 84
competence, 3, 11, 15, 20, 23, 37, 39, 42, 98
  functional, 94
  professional, 20–22
  technical, 21, 90
competencies, 6, 19, 70, 78, 91–92, 99, 111, 124
  improved, 6
  professional, 91
  technical, 91
competent mentors, 13
competitiveness, 14
competitors, 84
complements, 99, 134
complexities, 5–6, 23–24, 110, 115, 118
concept level, high, 60
conceptual level, 60
concerted effort, 36
confidence builder, 85, 98
confidence evaporates, 46
confident, 3, 73, 98, 108, 123, 129
confident communication, 90
confidential matters, 118
conflict, 22, 103–109, 130, 134
  interpersonal, 37
  relational, 128
conflict assessment, 105
conflict handling strategies, 103
conflict management, 101, 106
conflict resolution, 107
conflict situation, 104–108
  actual, 104
confrontation, 56, 107
connection, 37, 115, 124
  emotional, 38
  making, 116

negative, 41
new personal, 64
real, 33
right learning, 21
connect mentees, 26
conscious competence, 46
conscious incompetence, 46
consciousness, 24
consistency, 38
constant growth, 123
constant stimulation, 82
contacts, 110
  frequent, 20
  important, 115
  social, 116
content, 6, 51, 106, 116
context, 2, 32, 34, 44, 57, 71
  in-depth, 45
contextual understanding, 6
contract, 22, 102, 124, 130, 133
  psychological, 69
contracted period, 12
contracting, 17
contribution, 19, 36, 41, 54, 68, 80, 85, 93, 99, 105
  current, 79
  meaningful, 136
conversant, 22, 127
conversation descriptions, 65
conversation on career momentum/mobility, 75
conversation on purpose and vision, 66
conversation outcome/assignment, 70, 80, 86, 92, 99, 102, 112, 120
conversation process, 131
conversation questions, 133
conversations, 16–17, 30–36, 42–44, 47–48, 50–51, 56–57, 59–60, 64–65, 68–70, 78–79, 89–92, 95–102, 109–111, 115–119, 132–134

actionable, 31, 59
fitness, 92–93
forward-looking, 91
frequent, 87
great, 58
interactive, 43
meaningful, 59
right, 21
shift, 59
shifting, 132
single, 64
convey, 23–24, 48, 56
convictions, 118
cooperation, mutual, 47
cornerstone, 37, 100
corporate baggage, 9
corporate life, 84
courageous self-exploration, 53
CPAs (Critical Performance Areas), 14
creativity, 97, 134
credibility, 122
  building, 49
Critical Performance Areas (CPAs), 14
crucial conversations, 43, 66, 75, 83, 89, 96, 100, 109, 117
crucial mentoring conversations, 17
cultural background, 107
cultural fit, 123
cultural understanding, 11
culture, 6, 9, 11, 17–18, 23, 25, 41–42, 44, 50, 101
  stories strengthen, 48
  unique, 18, 23
current performance, 87, 119
  improving, 87
cycle, 129
  natural, 87

D

dangers, 90, 116, 123
deadlines, 35, 57
decisions, 4, 23–24, 30, 33–34, 71, 119
 hiring, 116
 life's, 68
 mentee's, 73
 wrong, 73
deepen, 33, 69, 108
deepen understanding, 46
delegates, 25, 37
deliberate efforts, 41
demonstrates, 105
demotivating, 84
demystifying, 31
department's outputs, 78
dependability, 38
depredation, 40
depth, 42–43, 115, 118, 125, 132
de-railers, 123
destructive interactions, 41
destructive relationship, 47
developing strengths, 98
development actions, 93
development activities, 92
 possible, 91
developmental assignments, 78
developmental goal, 57
development areas, 17, 98–99
 professional, 42
development journey, 5, 28, 110
 mentee's, 28
 personal, 86
development tool, 7, 18
 effective professional, 13
dialogue, 59
 open, 132
diplomacies, 56
direct organisational benefits, 13
disabilities, 25
disagreements, 57, 106–107, 128
 sharp, 107
disappointments, 22, 85
disapproval, 57
discernment, 10, 106
discipline, 4, 17, 68, 71
 mentee's, 73
discovery, 31, 68–69
dislikes, 106–107
diversity, 9, 11, 20, 50, 55, 101–102
dreams, 4, 27, 48, 67, 69, 72, 122, 133
dysfunctions, 59

E

economic factors, 24
educate senior members, 8
education, 25–26, 51, 76
educational interventions, 12
effective mentoring relationships, 42
egos, 9, 106
 employee's, 84
electronic detox, 35
emotional connotations, 48
emotional intelligence assessments, 135
emotions, 35, 48, 53, 101, 104–106, 117, 135
emphasise, 2–3, 53
employability, 20, 75–76, 79
 lifetime, 75
 mentee's, 132
employee development conversations, 93
employee engagement, 5
employee retention, 11
employees, 3, 6, 8, 11, 14, 18, 21, 69, 84, 87, 90, 93, 96–97
 best, 69
 core, 95
 good, 90
 high potential, 14
 longer, 96

employee's capability, 93
employers, 69, 76, 116
  potential, 75
employment, 69, 76
  finding, 106
  lifetime, 75
  previous, 71
encouragement, 6, 27, 41, 110
endeavours, 4
  corporate, 18
energy, 14, 21, 54, 59, 67, 115
  high, 59
engagement, 11, 24–25, 42, 118
enjoyment enthusiasm, 74
entrepreneur, 43
entrepreneurial creativity, 82
entrepreneurial skills, 8
entrust, 5, 110
environment, 11, 24, 42
  challenging, 60
  flexible, 7
  high trust, 39
  structured mentoring, 18
ethical issue, 49
evaluation, 36, 115
events, 24, 33–34, 50, 71, 73, 87
  charged, 48
  critical, 49
  important, 70
  negative, 71, 73
  newsworthy, 24
exchanges, 17, 36, 69
execution, 25, 42, 59, 133
executive coaching, 3
executive level, 93
executives, 19
  top-level, 8
expectations, 9, 16, 20, 39, 47, 60, 88, 105, 123, 129–130
  abstract, 130
  high, 41, 60, 122, 124
  managing, 130
  unrealistic, 22
experience, 15, 18, 21, 24–27, 31, 35, 45, 48, 73, 78–79, 104, 107, 129, 132–133, 136
experienced mentors, 22
experience fear, 60
expertise, 7, 22, 39, 123
  functional, 78
  specialised, 78
experts, 95, 98
  subject matter, 14, 26, 81
exposure, 7–9, 11, 23, 26–27, 72, 79–80, 124, 127, 133
  comprehensive, 30
  on-the-job, 26
  planned, 19, 127
eye for an eye mentality, 105

F

face-to-face interaction, 128
face-to-face practice, 5
facilitators, 5, 130
factual stories, 50
failures, 22, 56, 59, 98, 108, 110, 119, 129–130
fairness, 76
family therapist, 120
fear, 38, 40, 53, 60, 105, 120
  emotions inspire, 61
  strong, 107
feedback, 16, 26–27, 45–46, 53, 57, 86–89, 93, 95, 99–100, 102, 110, 123, 125, 135
  actionable, 60
  constructive, 86
  helpful, 85, 88, 134
  honest, 7, 9, 32, 53, 118
  negative, 86, 88
  preparing, 60
  quality, 133
  regular, 125

robust, 31
feelings, 38, 40–41, 56, 103–104, 117–118
  hard, 107
  people's, 118
  positive, 118
  suppressed, 120
financial background, strong, 67
financial difficulties, 119
financial rewards, 69, 87
fine-tune development strategies, 93
fitness, 43, 46, 66, 75, 77, 83, 89–90, 95–96, 100, 109, 117, 134
fitness freedom, 74
flawed assumptions, 96
focus areas, 25
  interlinked, 21
focus groups, 37
followers, 20, 116
force change, 55
forced marriages, 15
force managers, 15
formal mentoring, 12–16
formal mentoring initiative, 15
formal mentoring relationships, 17–18
formal relationships work, 18
formal/structured approach, 14
formal/structured mentoring, 10, 131
foundation, 54
  solid, 25, 130
framework, 17, 44
  common, 38
  enhanced, 28
  informal, 42
fulfilment, 20, 33
functional areas, 95
functions, 11, 21, 25, 55, 78
  current, 99
fundamentals, 21

G

gender, 41, 44, 50, 93, 101
gender perspectives, 9
generation, 6, 9, 20, 48, 50, 67, 101
  literate, 6
  younger, 8, 36, 69, 122
generational, 6, 9
globalisation highlights, 5
goal attainment, 3
golden rules, 106
graduate development, 14
grooming talent, 87
group, 27, 38, 94–95, 103, 108, 135
  ideal target, 95
  low performance, 95
  low potential, 94
  succession, 123
  talent bench, 95
growth, 14, 19, 28, 55, 80, 97, 125
  greatest, 97
  personal, 16
  professional, 15
growth experience, 132
guidance, 4, 38, 43, 77
guide, 18, 44, 48, 51, 69, 129, 133

H

habits, 55, 59
  rare, 40
  self-destructive, 27
handling conflict, 107
hard-gained experience, 19
health, 3, 71, 119
  good, 55
health insurance claims, 116
heart, 4, 14–15, 17, 40, 109
high achievers, 122–124
high performers, 125
holistic development, 21
holistic development blueprint, 26

honesty, 49, 51, 56
hurt feelings, 107

I

identifying career, 78
imbalances, 11
  demographic, 11
implications, 58
impressions, 36, 42, 57
improvement, 60, 85
  continuous, 46
incompetence, 90
independence, 21, 82
in-depth understanding, 32
indispensable circle, 109
individuals, 4, 10, 37–38, 53, 66–67, 75, 77, 81, 86, 89, 95, 102, 104, 112, 116
  experienced, 4
  like-minded, 110
  trusted, 27
  value-adding, 22
individuals highlights, 83
industry, 2, 7, 76, 78
informal check-ins, 87
informal interactions, 4
informal mentoring, 10, 12–13
informal mentoring relationships, 12, 20
informal relationships, 16
information, 6, 16, 25, 34, 36, 76, 88, 103, 112–113, 118, 120, 136
  gathering, 36
information age, 6
information overload, 6
innovation, 7, 22, 97, 134
  continuous, 23
insecurities, 126
inspire, 3, 22, 48, 50–51, 59
  purposely, 39
inspire trust, 39

institutionalising mentoring, 14
intelligence, 117
  emotional, 5, 8, 10, 81, 101–102
intentional effort, 31, 90, 124
intentional mentoring, 21, 26–27, 95
intentional relationship, 19
intentional response, 49
International Coach Federation, 2
intimate understanding, 32
intimidating, 51, 99
isolation, 105–106

J

job coaching, 7
job interview, 46
job rotation, 26
Johari Window, 102–103
Johari Window perspectives, 103
journey, 110
  personal, 52, 71, 119
  professional, 70
judgemental, 40
judgment, perceived, 57
junior staff members, 8
justifications, 112

K

knowledge, 3–4, 6–7, 21–22, 25–26, 33, 36, 76, 78, 111, 131, 134
  economy, 6, 78
  sharing, 6, 15
  transfer, 5

L

leader/manager, 59
leaders, 3, 6–7, 9, 52–53, 65, 85, 90
  executive, 3
  inspiring, 50
leadership, 39, 44, 49, 76, 91, 93, 95, 102

servant, 49, 59
leadership ambitions, 8
leadership challenges, 23
leadership competencies, 90
leadership development, 11
leadership feedback, 9
leadership initiatives, 95
leadership pipeline, 14
leadership requirements, 42
leadership role, 125
leadership skills, 7
 strong, 78
leadership style, 9, 102
learner response, 45–46
learners, 5, 26, 44–46
 active, 5
learning, 2–3, 5, 11, 16, 19, 21, 25, 27–28, 31, 33, 35, 44–45, 125, 132
 collaborative, 21
 continuous, 7
 formal, 26
 inter-generational, 11
 leverage, 18
 on-the-job, 27
learning activities, 26, 91
 expanding, 26
learning agility, 93
learning experience, 132
learning process, 5, 69
learning spectrum, 26
lessons, 9, 15, 33, 39, 48–50, 80, 85, 131, 133
 important, 49
level exposure, 93
leverage, 99, 110, 112, 124
leveraging intentional mentoring, 27
life choices, 69, 73
life coaching, 3
life decisions, 70
life lessons, 49, 119
lifeline, 71

lifeline relationships, 26
lifelong mentor, 5, 110
lifelong passion area, 98
life purpose, 67
life skill, 129
life stories, 19, 70
 personal, 119
lifestyle, 78, 83
life timeline, 70–71
limitations, 41
line-manager, 22, 47
line-manager relationships, 84
line managers, 19, 21, 93, 100
 current, 86
listener, 48, 50, 102
long-term jobs/projects, 122
low expectations, 129

M

management, 4, 11, 90
 defined relationship, 101
management consultant, 65
management experience, 9
management level, 11
management practices, 13
management team, 114, 123
management tool, 11
managerial competence, 81
managerial levels, 78, 115
managers, 3, 7–9, 12–13, 30, 37, 64, 78, 81, 84, 87, 90, 93–95, 127, 136
 best, 77
 engineering, 90
 financial, 90
 project, 86
managing relationships, 16
match mentors, 13, 15
maturity, 65, 109
 emotional, 58
 questions verifying, 128

Index

measurable elements, 133
measurable outcomes, 12
measurement, 10, 13
mentee acts, 69
mentee alienates, 100
mentee answer, 133
mentee master, 101
mentee network, 110
mentee process, 57
mentees, 15–28, 31–35, 40–48, 55–60, 64–65, 69–71, 73, 77–81, 84–88, 90–92, 96–104, 109–115, 118–120, 122–127, 129–136
  best, 44
  confident, 123
mentees battle, 25
mentees in informal relationships, 20
mentees set, 126
mentees strategies, 23
mentee's development plan, 85
mentee's efforts, 131
mentee's interaction, 86
mentee's issues, 129
mentee's opinion, 123
mentee's performance, 84, 86, 134
mentee's preferences, 81
mentee's profile, 135
mentee's relationship, 104
mentee's situation, 65
mentee's talents, 97
mentor contracting, 126
mentor contribution, 45–46
mentoring, 2–21, 23, 25–27, 34, 38, 53, 59, 64, 72, 84, 122, 125, 132, 136
  effective, 21, 59
  modern, 39
mentoring and coaching, 2
mentoring context, 35
mentoring conversation, actual, 49
mentoring conversation grants, 33
mentoring conversations, 2, 4, 6–8, 10, 12, 14, 16–18, 20, 22, 24, 26, 28–61, 63–124, 126, 130–136
mentoring conversations broaden, 33
mentoring efforts, 19
mentoring endeavour, 124
mentoring engagements, 13
mentoring expectations, 130
mentoring experience, 33
mentoring harnesses, 11
mentoring networks, 32
mentoring paradigm, 6
mentoring partner, 49, 57
mentoring process, 60
mentoring programmes, 14
  corporate, 5
  formal, 5
mentoring relationship
  healthy, 16
  unique, 79
mentoring relationships, 9–10, 12, 14, 16–18, 20, 25, 31, 36–37, 47, 50, 59–60, 111, 113, 118, 120
mentoring role, 14, 132
mentoring session, 35
mentoring skills, 124
mentor phrase, 125
mentor revolves, 4
mentors, 4–5, 12–28, 31–33, 35–42, 44–49, 52–58, 60, 64–65, 68–69, 84–85, 95–97, 109–111, 117–118, 122–127, 129–134
  authentic, 33, 53
  informal, 30
  intentional, 21, 27, 45
  potential, 43
mentor's charm, 52
mentors expose, 134
mentorship endeavour, 20
mentorship relationship, 21
mentor's mentoring approach, 126
mentors pass, 4

mentors reap, 33
mentor's responsibility, 39, 126
mentor's role, 44
mentors savour, 4
metaphors, 48, 50, 99
methodologies, 2
millennials, 6–8, 36
mindset, 22
  positive, 22, 34
  progressive, 23
model, 25, 102, 124
  classroom, 25
  self-explanatory, 102
modern mentors, 26
moments, 4, 33, 35, 47, 52, 71, 118–119
  greatest, 101
  high-stakes, 44
  important, 71
  key teaching, 133
  special, 35
motivation, 20, 22, 47, 79, 103
  fundamental human, 77
motivator, 81
motives, 51, 57, 81

N

narratives, 51
  sharing, 48
navigating, 8, 42
negative publicity, 116
negative relationships, 46
negative way, 24
networking, 111, 115
  social, 116
network map, 114
network relationship, 115
networks, 4, 6, 8, 26–27, 43, 83, 89, 96, 100, 109, 111–112, 114–115, 117, 124, 133–134
  credible, 111
  extended, 111, 113, 134
  mentee's, 114
non-profitable relationship, 55
non-profit organisation, 67
non-verbal cues, 128
nurtures, 26, 111, 133
nurturing, 19, 27
nurturing interpersonal relationships, 103

O

objective person, 51
objectivity, 105
observations, 27, 48–49, 57–58
  direct, 57
office morale, 9
on-the-job implementation, 26
open-mindedness, 43
openness, 16, 19, 36, 56, 119, 130
operational challenges, 64
operational efficiencies, 17
operational positions, critical, 14
operational requirements, 21
organisational benefits, 13
organisational bureaucracy, 23
organisational challenges, 18
organisational mission, 68
organisational politics and perceptions, 120
organisational purpose, 8
organisation calibrates talent, 91
organisation calibrate talent/fitness, 93
organisations, 2–3, 6–7, 9–12, 14–15, 17–18, 20, 23–26, 30, 32, 68–71, 77–78, 86–87, 90, 92–93, 96–97
organisation's mission, 69
organisation's success, 87
organisation's top talent, 95
orientation, 12, 81
over-ambition, 122

overloading, 18
ownership, 16, 44, 58, 82

P

participants, 26, 34, 38, 131
participation, 19
parties, 10, 15–16, 18–19, 31–32, 34, 36, 64, 105
partner, 70, 111, 116
  valued, 67
passions, 4, 67, 76, 83, 99, 129, 136
  personal, 97
  unwavering, 43
passive observers, 53
passive recipient, 5
path, 55, 110, 124
  real, 26, 110
  single, 71
patience, 19, 69, 106
paying attention, 24
paying compliments, 88
peer mentoring, 5–6
  leveraged, 6
peer relationships, 22
peers, 5–6, 30, 57, 104
  new, 43
perceptions, 9, 22, 101, 104, 120, 123
  deep-seated, 101
  possible, 88
performance, 2, 7, 32, 37, 43, 45, 60, 66, 75, 78, 83–87, 89–91, 93–96, 100, 133–134
  consistent, 110
  high, 87
  near-perfect, 97
  past, 87
performance appraisals, 42
performance conversations, 85, 87
  authentic, 86
performance enhancer, 85
performance issues, 134

performance management, 84–85, 87, 134
performance management paradigm, 87
performance management system, 87
  organisation's, 84
performers, 84, 94–95
  average, 94
  best, 77
  consistent, 95
  star, 95, 123
persistence, 68
person, 5, 33, 36, 55, 65, 81, 88, 97, 103, 105, 107–108, 110, 128–129
  connected, 112
personal attributes, 76
personal circumstances, 120
personal development, 7, 11, 16, 44, 60, 103
personal difficulties, 40
personal experience, 30, 119
personal goals, 3
personality, 101, 135
personality types, 106, 135
personal judgments, 57
personal life, 26, 83
personal losses, 71, 119
personal mistakes, 40
Personal network map, 114
personal privacy, 116
personal relationships, 3
personal renewal, 20
personal sacrifice, 92
personal values, 68
  common, 73
person's background, 107
person's interests, 88
person's spectacles, 107
perspectives, 32, 55–56, 64, 106–108, 133
  mentee's, 123
pipeline, 54

149

company's, 12
planned reaction, 106
platforms, 6, 9, 118, 128
　media, 128
　social, 10
plots employee performance, 93
point, 49–51, 56, 61, 65, 105, 112
　timing, 65
　turning, 49
polarisation, 36
political influence, 112
political landscape, 16
politics, 23
possible mentoring conversation, 112
possible mentoring story, 70, 80, 86, 92, 99, 102, 119
power, 53, 58, 77, 88, 129, 135
practice accountability, 39
practice vulnerability, 54
preach, 53
predictability, 40
predictions, 24, 90
preferred way, 135
prejudice models behaviour, 41
prerequisites, 16, 34, 80, 92
prerequisites dovetail, 8
presentation, 46, 57, 86, 126–127
　important, 47
pressure environments, 126
pressures, 35, 64, 135
prestige, 77, 91
priorities, 16, 25, 68–69, 81
　critical, 64
　daily, 36
　personal, 132
prioritise, 73, 115
privilege, 54, 66, 122
　massive, 136
proactiveness, 133
proactive role, 90
problem solving, 19, 27, 32, 81
productive mentoring relationship, 42
productive relationships, 32
professional assistance, 130
professional bodies definition, 2
professional career identity, enhanced, 20
professional conduct, 23
professional development, 31–33
professional goals, 70
professional identity, 79, 133
professionalism, 10
professional life, 71, 77
professional relationships, improved, 11
professional supervision, 17
profitable mentoring relationships, 13, 16, 20, 42, 118, 132, 135
profitable mentorship relationship, 19
profitable relationships, 14, 19, 37, 59, 101, 110
programme, 9, 18
　management development, 130
　structured mentoring, 14
programme administrator, 15
progression, 91, 123
project meeting, 35
project-related query, 30
projects, 3, 24–25, 27, 30, 47, 54
projects finish, 87
project team, 27
project work, 35
promises, 30, 37, 39–40, 42, 53, 111
promotion, 5, 30, 77–78, 95, 132
promotors, 39
protective communication, 37
public persona, 53
purpose
　corporate, 68
　individual, 68
　mentee's, 68, 133
　mutual, 48
purposefulness, 69

Index

Q

qualified practitioner, 102
qualities, 2, 4, 16, 22, 37, 41, 43, 52, 68, 87, 89, 102, 115, 118, 124
qualities/strengths, 41
questions
  common, 77
  creative, 127
  hard, 69
  mentee's, 129
  possible, 44
  reflective, 127
  right, 32, 64–65
  searching, 127
  suggested, 65
questions focus, 58
questions forms, 65

R

readiness, 65, 90–91, 93, 105, 123, 134
  mentee's, 92
realisation, 106
realities, 18, 23, 33, 118
  organisational, 80
reciprocal contributions, 34, 36
reciprocal mentoring, 8
reciprocal mentoring relationship, 36
reciprocal outcomes, 19
recognition, 20, 33, 77–78, 89, 91
recommendations, 32, 135
reflective process, 28, 132
relationship challenges, 119
relationship management skills, 103
relationship network, 115
  mentee's mentoring, 113
relationships, challenging, 122
religion, 41, 43–44, 50, 101
reputation, 39, 53, 56, 76, 106–107
resentments, 36, 55, 105
resources, 54, 80, 85, 111, 115, 134

natural, 96
responsibilities, 16, 21, 23, 27, 34, 44, 58, 60, 79, 81, 92, 95, 122, 126, 129–130
résumé, 22, 30, 76, 80, 116
return on relationship, 10, 17
reverse mentoring, 8–9, 36, 53
reverse mentoring initiatives, 9
reverse mentoring relationships, 9
review employee plans, 93
review meeting support, 18
reward, 18, 78, 90, 129
risks, 38, 82, 90
  potential, 56
role models, 4, 130
  perfect, 130
role players, 15, 31, 51, 86, 104, 111–112, 115, 134

S

selection process, 12
self-assurance, 98
self-awareness, 2, 42, 46, 69, 103, 106, 136
  developing, 53
self-belief, 100
  elevated, 122
self-esteem, low, 71
self-fulfilling prophecies, 129
self-learning, 132
self-management, 8, 106
self-reflection, 35–36
  critical, 35
self-regard, 100
sensitivity, 41, 58
setbacks, 22
set career goals, 133
shared goals, 20
shared interests, 20
shifting responsibility, 56
short term goals, 70

151

skilful mentors, 25
skilled careers, 5
skill levels, 3
skills, 3–4, 7, 9, 21–22, 25, 39, 42, 46,
    76, 79, 81, 97, 99–101, 123, 126
  core, 79, 131
  delicate, 126
  developing, 87, 97
  important, 104
  listening, 8
  managerial, 39
  mentee's, 19
  portable, 78
  recombine, 78
  technical, 7, 39
  workplace, 91
skillsets, 126
skills transfer, 11
social awareness, 106
social media, 8, 111, 114, 116
social media and virtual platforms, 5
social media interfaces, 9
social media platforms, 9
social media sites, 116
social support, 6
society, 14, 70
solutions, 24, 31, 105, 129
  finding, 23
sophistication, 23
specialists, 30, 135
  behavioural, 120
sponsors, 32, 110–111, 114, 123, 134
  potential, 123
sponsorship, 23
sponsor's radar, 110
spontaneity, 18
stability, 77, 81–82
staff, 3, 8, 53, 84, 87, 90
  multiplying the talents of, 59
standards, 108
  dislike, 82
  high, 39

statement, 53, 64, 66
  personal purpose, 70
status quo, 126
stories, 48–53, 65, 71, 86, 92, 112,
    116, 119
  great, 48
  personal, 33, 49
storytellers, 48, 51
storyteller's secret, 50
storytelling, 48–51
  power of, 48, 52
strategies, central, 13
strength finder assessments, 99, 135
strengths, 11, 46, 96–99, 106, 123,
    129, 134
  complements, 99
  conversation on, 96, 99
  highlight, 17
  individual's, 90
  mentee's, 98–99
  personal, 99
  playing to your, 99
  securing strong bench, 92
stretched goals, 95
strong company values, 7
strong disputes, 107
structure, 10, 12, 14, 17–18, 77
structured approach, 15
structured mentoring, 12
structured mentoring relationships,
    18
structured process, 13
structured relationship, 4
structured strategic business
    initiative, 10
subjective bosses, 84
subordinates, 5, 104
succession planning, 11, 93, 122
support career growth, 130
support networks, 6
  informal, 53
survival, 50, 99

long-term, 87
suspicion, 36
  risk raising, 57
sustainability, 12, 14–15, 67, 99
sustainable change, 132

T

tacit information, 6
tacit knowledge, 10, 44
talent bench, 12, 92
talent calibration, 93
talented mentee, 23
talented young individuals, 14
talent grid, 92, 94
talent management, 5
talent pool, 123
teachers, 3, 19, 35, 37
  good, 90
team, 85, 98
  cohesive, 90
team management skills, 39
team members, 9, 70
team roles, 94
team work, 101
technical/functional competence, 81
technologies, 22, 35, 125, 128
  changing, 7
  disruptive, 23
technology awareness, 9
temper tantrums, 53
terminology, 59
territory, 99, 134
testify, 4, 14, 18
themed analogies, 50
thinking
  box, 133
  critical, 34
  picture, 8
  strategic, 90
  unbroken, 24
  whole-brain, 135

thinking styles, 101
timeline, 50, 68, 71, 73
timeline exercise, 73
tools, 3, 13, 25, 48, 93, 111, 127, 132, 135–136
  authentic, 11
  brain profiling, 135
  great, 102
  proactive, 91
  reliable, 135
  social/development, 50
  strategic, 93
topics, 22, 32, 34–35, 40, 42, 44–45, 48, 60, 68–69, 112, 120, 125, 129, 134–135
  contentious, 108
  possible, 9
  sensitive, 16
  tricky, 31
toughest relationships, 102
track record, 76
  individual's, 76
training, 12, 25–27, 95, 100
  formal, 26
transfer knowledge, 36
transformation, 59–60
  professional, 59
transparency, 40, 119
trends, 8, 10, 14, 27
  global, 23
  organisational, 24
trust, 10, 20, 36–39, 41, 47, 87, 112, 118, 124
  authentic, 34, 37
  breaks/erodes, 37
  cultivator of, 40–41
  high levels of, 16, 19
  level of, 37–39
  low, 37
  mutual, 4, 130
  promotors of, 39, 41–42
trusted collection, 110

153

trusted relationships, 110
trusting, 122
trusting relationships, 8, 38
truth, 15, 25, 50, 54, 67, 119
  fundamental, 97, 134

U

ultimate anti-career guide, 75
ultimate goal, 59
unconscious competence, 46
unconscious incompetence, 45
underperformers, 94–95
undetermined period, 67
uninterrupted sleep, 55
unquestionable benefits, 10, 12

V

value alignment, 73
value proposition, 124
values, 5–8, 10–11, 17–19, 32–33, 40, 44–45, 47, 53–54, 56–58, 64–65, 68–71, 73–74, 79, 81, 111
  common, 68, 74
  corporate, 68
  organisation's, 73
viewpoints, 34, 50, 106
virtual platforms, 5
vision, 66–67, 69, 72, 79, 133
vulnerabilities, 41, 53–54, 118
  real life conflict, 134

W

weaknesses, 41, 53, 97, 99–100
  greatest, 97
  mentee's, 99
  minimise, 134
weaknesses drain confidence, 99
wealth, 74, 136
  great, 96

well-intended pre-meditated actions, 19
well-planned effort, 127
wisdom, 23, 32–34, 48, 74, 106, 111, 126
  institutional, 19
  territorial, 23–24
words, 6, 40, 88, 107, 127
  hurtful, 128
  spoken, 88
work disappointments, 22
work environment, 11, 26
work experience, 26
work off-shore, 78
work performance, 22, 85
workplace, 9, 25, 81
workplace guidance, 23
workplace knowledge, 91
work pressures, 6
work-role effectiveness, 23

www.ingramcontent.com/pod-product-compliance
Lightning Source LLC
Chambersburg PA
CBHW051101160426
43193CB00010B/1275